D09955848

CHEAP RAW MATERIAL

CHEAP RAW MATERIAL

MILTON MELTZER

VIKING

To all those who seek to protect the health
and safety of young workers
—M.M.

Grateful acknowledgment is made for permission to
reproduce the following illustrations:

pages 5, 15, 18 (top), 27, 31: The Granger Collection; pages 18 (bottom), 40,
50, 67 (top): The Bettmann Archive; pages 57 (top and bottom), 67 (bottom),
72 (top and bottom): National Child Labor Committee / Lewis Hine; page 80
(top and bottom): UPI/Bettmann Newsphotos; pages 85, 90, 116: © Earl
Dotter, 1991; page 98: © Dani Steele, 1990; page 105: UN Photo 145232/Jean
Pierre Laffont; page 120: Junior Achievement of New York; page 127: Job
Corps; page 132: © Sean Sprague/Impact Visuals 1990; page 134: UN PHOTO
148,001/Jean Pierre Laffont; page 143 (top): © Mev Puleo, Impact Visuals 1989;
page 143 (bottom): Philip Decker, Impact Visuals; © 1984, Philip Decker

VIKING
Published by the Penguin Group
Penguin Books USA Inc., 375 Hudson Street, New York, New York 10014, U.S.A.
Penguin Books Ltd, 27 Wrights Lane, London W8 5TZ, England
Penguin Books Australia Ltd, Ringwood, Victoria, Australia
Penguin Books Canada Ltd, 10 Alcorn Avenue, Toronto, Ontario, Canada M4V 3B2
Penguin Books (N.Z.) Ltd, 182-190 Wairau Road, Auckland 10, New Zealand
Penguin Books Ltd, Registered Offices: Harmondsworth, Middlesex, England

First published in 1994 by Viking, a division of Penguin Books USA Inc.

1   3   5   7   9   10   8   6   4   2

Copyright © Milton Meltzer, 1994
All rights reserved

LIBRARY OF CONGRESS CATALOGING-IN-PUBLICATION DATA
Meltzer, Milton
Cheap raw material : how our youngest workers are
exploited and abused / by Milton Meltzer.   p.   cm.
Includes bibliographical references.
ISBN 0-670-83128-X
1. Children—Employment—United States.
2. Children—Employment—Law and
legislation—United States.   I. Title.
HD6250.U3M45   1994   331.3′4′0973—dc20   93-31478   CIP

Printed in U.S.A.
Set in 11 pt. Bembo

CONTENTS

Introduction

Do you have a job? After school? Weekends? In summertime?

If you do, you know you're not alone among young people.

Six out of every ten twelfth graders and over three out of ten ninth graders work. Today, in the United States, about five million young people ages fourteen to eighteen work sometime during the year.

And thousands much younger—kids of only seven or eight or nine—work, too. They put in long hours, for low pay, interrupting their education and suffering accidents and even death.

Not long ago a reporter for *The Boston Globe* traveled around America to see what was happening to children and teenagers who work. When he came home months later, he wrote that:

> They live in poverty and neglect as they harvest our food, work in hundreds of dingy factories stitching "Made in America" tags onto our clothes, assemble cheap jewelry in trailer homes and tenements, operate dangerous machines in restaurant kitchens and neighborhood stores. In town after town, they serve our fast food meals late at night, prepare our muffins and coffee early in the morning.
>
> Often they are scalded and burned, sliced up by food machines, exposed to pesticides in the field and choking fumes in the factory. They fall and fracture their backs, and break their arms and hands frequently, delivering and picking up things for us. Sometimes, they are left badly maimed or disfigured for life.
>
> Sometimes, they are killed.
>
> Nearly all the time, they get tired, miss school and are ignored.

The reporter concluded that "America's children are among the nation's most widely exploited workers." He called this "a national shame."

Why does it happen?

In answering these questions, I have used numbers—hundreds, thousands, millions—to give some statistical measure of the seriousness of what this book deals with.

But such figures rarely touch the heart. If readers could only *see* each young worker, if they could *know* that boy or this girl, then they would be able to grasp the meaning of the large numbers. That is why, wherever possible in telling this story, I have let young people who work tell their story in their own words.

Children Have Always Worked

Children have always worked.

From the beginning of human history, even the very young did their share of work in the family. It was expected that they would help their parents however they could: foraging for food, herding animals, raising crops, doing household chores. And as they grew older, they helped to craft both useful and decorative objects. Children worked with one or both parents, sheltered by their care and learning from their experience.

But when slavery developed, way back in ancient times, children captured in war or bought on the slave market were held in bondage. A slave became another's property, owned legally by someone who had the sole right to that property.

When a noted Roman, Cato the Elder (234–149 B.C.) retired, he invested profitably in slaves. He bought a great

A slave market in ancient Rome where thousands of the white inhabitants of Britain were sold, from a nineteenth-century engraving.

many people the Roman legions had captured in war. His biggest deals were for cheap children, for he could have them trained to some trade or craft and then sell them at a high price and make lots of money.

In most schools and textbooks, the impression is conveyed that slavery was an experience of black people. But the historical record proves that people of every color—white, black, brown, yellow, red—have been the victims of slavery. The Romans enslaved thousands of the white inhabitants of Britain known as "Angles." In the slave markets of Rome in the sixth century A.D., blond, blue-eyed boys and girls could be seen awaiting sale.

Later, in the ninth century, the Vikings sold tens of thousands of captive whites to the Arabs in Spain. Many of them were boys to be trained for the militia and girls to be placed in harems. In 1212, thousands of little boys and girls took part in the Children's Crusade to free the Holy Land from the Moslems. But the youthful crusaders, most of them under twelve, were kidnapped by slave dealers and sold for labor in Egypt.

Young girls were commonly traded on the slave markets. In 1393, a rich Tuscan, Francesco Datini, wrote to his business agent in Genoa: "Pray buy for me a little slave girl, young and sturdy and of good stock, strong and able to work hard . . . so that I can bring her up in my own way. She will learn quicker and I shall get better service out of her."

In the fourteenth and fifteenth centuries, white slaves captured on the north coast of the Black Sea in Russia were sold in Italy, Spain, Egypt, and the Mediterranean islands. When the English general Oliver Cromwell invaded Ireland in the seventeenth century, his troops seized more than a hundred thousand men, women, and children and shipped them to the West Indies, where they were sold into slavery.

The roots of the abuse of children in America for financial profit go back to the time of Columbus, when the nations of Europe began to seek wealth and power through planting colonies abroad. The promoters of colonization (especially the British) figured on using children from the beginning. It would be good for boys and girls of twelve and under, they said, to be kept from idleness by shipping them to America, where they could be put to work making things for profit.

During the 1600s, these children of the poor lived a bare existence in the countryside or tried to survive in the crowded city of London. Perhaps two-thirds of them died before the age of four of malnutrition or during epidemics. The survivors often lost one or both parents to illness or accident and became part of a floating population of uncared-for children.

When the first British colony in Virginia was being planned, its investors arranged with the city of London in 1619 to have a hundred homeless white children picked up on the streets and sent to the colony for sale to the planters as laborers, thus "redeeming so many poor souls from misery and ruin." If any resisted, London's Privy Council authorized the Virginia Company to "imprison, punish and dispose of any of those children upon any disorder by them committed."

Hunting for white slaves became a thriving business in Britain. The press-gangs, as the groups of slave hunters were called, operated with the quiet approval of wealthy Britons, who feared the rapid increase of the rebellious poor. Organized raids were made upon English, Scottish, and Welsh people, young and old. The profits were split between the press-gangs and the shipmasters.

Children tagged as "vagrants" or "beggars" were in great danger. A British law in 1664 permitted their arrest and shipment overseas to the colonies. Judges got half the profits from their sale, with another slice going into the king's treasury.

Merchants, shippers, and even magistrates conspired to profit by the helplessness of children. Peter Williamson, himself the victim of a kidnapping, gave a detailed account of the almost unbelievable greed of such people. In 1743, while a poor child in the Scottish port of Aberdeen, playing on a wharf one day, he was lured aboard a nearby ship by two men and carried off with sixty-nine other boys and girls to America, where they were sold as slaves.

In 1757, having managed to gain his freedom, Williamson returned to Britain and began a one-man crusade to end the evil of the illegal trade in children. He wrote a popular book about his experiences, fearlessly naming names of the guilty. The result? He was found guilty of libel by an Aberdeen court, he was fined and thrown into jail, and his book was publicly burned.

If you have read Robert Louis Stevenson's popular novel *Kidnapped,* you may not have realized it is based on the true story of a boy. James Annesley was kidnapped and sold into slavery in America. The guilty person was his uncle, a nobleman who arranged the crime in order to remove the child's challenge to the nobleman's inheritance of his brother's property. The boy endured thirteen years of brutal treatment in America and almost died before he made his way back home to Scotland. His memoir was the basis of the Stevenson story. But the thousands of poor children who suffered the same harsh treatment in the colonies rarely came to public attention.

The word *kidnapper*—or "kid-nabber"—seems to have been coined in Britain in the 1670s to describe those who captured and sold white children into slavery.

Once the captives were aboard ship for the Atlantic voyage, their horrors increased. They were kept below deck, often held in chains, for the long journey of nine to twelve weeks. Labor historian Foster R. Dulles writes that they "experienced discomforts and sufferings . . . that paralleled the cruel hardships undergone by Negro slaves in the notorious Middle Passage. . . . Young children seldom survived the horrors." On one trip, thirty-two children died of hunger or disease and were thrown into the ocean.

But weren't these passengers—children or adults—"indentured servants"? That's what the history textbooks call them. That phrase refers to people who came to America under a contract of indenture with ship captains, merchants, or contractors who paid for their passage. Their indenture pledged them to provide their labor for a limited number of years, in return for the promise of some free land at the end of their service. Most of these people were ages twenty-one to twenty-four. Younger ones were often the children of indentured families.

But a truth much ignored is that a great number of the original white immigrants did not come here of their own free will. They were deceived, lured, kidnapped, and even brought in chains to colonial America.

Many went of their own accord. Living conditions were bad for so many people of Britain and Europe that they were eager to emigrate to America. They hoped that in the New World they'd find a refuge from poverty and anxiety. Unable to pay for their passage, they signed indentures. When ships carried them into American ports, buyers came on deck to look over the human "merchandise." One indentured servant wrote these lines of verse to describe what happened:

Examining like horses, if we're sound. . . .
Some felt our hands and viewed our legs and
feet,
And made us walk, to see if we were
complete. . . .
If any liked our look, our limbs, our trade,
The captain then a good advantage made.

The commerce in human beings aboard these ships sometimes resulted in the separation of parents and children. In a report on his experience coming to America from Germany as an indentured servant in 1750, Gottlieb Mittelberger said that "many parents must barter and sell their children as if they were cattle. Since the fathers and mothers often do not know where or to what masters their children are to be sent, it frequently happens that after leaving the vessel, parents and children do not see each other for years on end, or even for the rest of their lives."

Legally the white people were not sold into lifetime servitude. Rather, the contract of indenture was bought by a buyer looking for someone to work for him for a specified number of years. Buyers got a great bargain, for within a year the servant's labor usually repaid the cost of the contract. The remaining years of labor were all profit for the master.

The seller sold the work contracts for the best price he could get. For children, that price was low. They were neither strong nor skilled and were of use mainly as house servants during their early years. Paid nothing for their labor and given no formal training, the indentured servants usually lived in the master's household.

Besides those children who came to the colonies as indentured servants, there was another group of children, those whose poor families couldn't support them in America. These children, as well as orphans, were placed as indentured servants by local officials responsible for care of the poor. Children of both groups served in the homes of prosperous townfolk—merchants, lawyers, bankers. As the historian Janet Wells Greene writes, the children "built fires, carried wood and water, emptied chamber pots, swept and scrubbed floors, washed dishes, polished silver, peeled potatoes and other vegetables, helped with cooking and washing, mending and marketing. Boys tended horses; girls learned plain sewing."

Whether as indentured servants or slaves, and in both North and South, children had no control over their personal lives. Laws provided harsh treatment for runaways. Legislators, themselves of the master class, often stretched out the terms of servitude. Break a rule and your service was lengthened. Have a baby (often forced upon a girl by the master himself) and it added more years to your service. And these children—"bastards," they were called—were bound over to the mother's master for a period of thirty-one years. Later this was reduced to a "mere" twenty-one years for boys and eighteen for girls. Often servants who completed their contracts were not given the money or tools or clothing that their contracts promised.

Some remained in what can only be called slavery for twenty, thirty, even forty years. As the end of a term of servitude neared, the master might turn the screws on working conditions even tighter, hoping the worker would run away, so that when he was caught, seven more years could be added to his servitude.

If a servant disobeyed the master, the law called for physical punishment. One traveler noted that he saw a servant beaten on the head with a cane until the blood flowed. A boy in New Jersey drowned himself rather than take another brutal beating from his master. In Maryland, John Dandy beat a boy to death and flung his body into a creek. There are thousands of such cases in the colonial records. Justice? Rarely were masters tried for such crimes. If they were, they were usually acquitted or let off lightly.

Apprentices made up a different class of child labor in the colonies. The new settlements counted on everybody working, whether child or adult. The governors of the colonies ruled that it was the child's duty to work and the father's legal obligation to prepare children for a useful occupation.

Although children began working at the age of six, it was usually at age ten to fourteen that fathers chose an occupation for them. Parents volunteered their children for apprenticeship. But children who were orphaned or poor or neglected were compelled into apprenticeship by the local officials. Such boys and girls had little choice of master or trade. A standard agreement required the master to provide the apprentice with meals, clothes, and a place to live and to teach the child the craft. In return, the apprentice was to work loyally for the master, do whatever was asked, live where told to, and remain with the master till the age of twenty-one.

In America, anyone could call himself a master craftsman

and take on apprentices. For the apprentices, to learn a top-rated craft or trade meant they could one day earn a good living. The agreement between master and apprentice also obligated the master to instruct apprentices in reading, writing, and simple arithmetic. If a master was illiterate or unwilling to teach, he was supposed to send apprentices to school and pay their tuition.

Like indentured servants, apprentices ran away from their masters. The laws forced runaways, when caught, to serve double the time of their absence. If they refused to obey orders, they could be sent to jail until they agreed to serve again faithfully. The newspapers frequently carried advertisements for the return of fugitive apprentices or servants. One master, in these lines of verse, advertised in the *Pennsylvania Gazette* of March 6, 1776, that his apprentice boy Tom had fled:

> *This present instant on the fourteenth day,*
> *My apprentice boy did run away;*
> *Thomas Stillenger he is called by name,*
> *His indenture further testifies the same;*
> *He had always been a vexatious lad,*
> *One reason why he is so meanly clad;*
> *To describe the rest I am not inclined,*
> *Cloth for a jacket he left behind;*
> *Of apple pies he took with him but five,*
> *For to preserve himself alive;*
> *Three quarter dollars are missed of late,*
> *Which perhaps he took to pay his freight;*
> *Believe him not if you be wise,*

He is very artful in telling lies;
For which I whipt him, I thought severe,
But did not make him shed one tear.
Whoever doth him safely secure
Of a reward they may be sure,
Six-pence at least I do propose
To give for him with all his clothes;
Or clear me of him forever and mine.
And his indentures away I will sign;
Now to inform you further still,
I keep a saw and fulling mill;
In East-Fallowfield township
And Chester County is the place of my abode,
I subscribe my name until the same, and that is
William Moode

Benjamin Franklin is undoubtedly the best-known American to have mastered a trade as an apprentice. His father apprenticed him, at the age of ten, in his own shop making soap and candles—honest and useful work, but stinking, dreary, and boring. Young Ben worked twelve to fourteen hours a day, six days a week, and he hated it. After two years, his father gave up on passing the trade to his son. Ben entered the printshop of his half brother James. He did the usual apprentice chores: swept the office and shop, got up early to build a fire, fetched water, ran errands. And when James let him, he learned to set type and use the press. Always devoted to the printed word, Ben didn't mind the hard work and the long hours it took to master a highly skilled trade, for he loved it. Quickly he became an expert in a craft he would never tire of, even when he went on to become a world-renowned scientist and a founding father of the new American nation.

So far we've talked about the white children who worked in colonial America.

What about the black children?

The young Benjamin Franklin as a printer's apprentice.

Bargains Black and White

Children were among the twelve million Africans brought to the New World in chains during the two hundred years when the Atlantic slave trade was at its peak. The slave trade began with the Portuguese in the year 1441. But as profits mounted, the Dutch, the English, the French, the Spanish, and the Danes became competitors. Eventually the British outstripped all their rivals to take over more than half the total trade.

Slavery itself was an ancient custom throughout the African continent. It existed there as early as the year 1000 B.C. In most cases, slaves were captives taken in wars between African peoples. The Europeans who launched the Atlantic slave trade generally bought slaves from African owners or dealers, carried them to the Americas, and resold them.

The men who brought the slaves from Africa were a mixed lot—Christians and cutthroats, gentlemen and pirates, speculators and adventurers, seamen and surgeons. Overcrowding their ships was the obvious way to raise the rate of profit on a voyage. Slaves were wedged into ships' holds like logs and chained. There was almost no room to sit, stand, or lie down. The holds were dank, filthy, slimy, and they stank. Some slaves who did not die of contagious diseases at sea chose suicide rather than captivity, and some slaves revolted. The death rate from these voyages was staggering, perhaps 25 percent.

With the growth of plantations in the New World, the need for slave labor increased enormously. As demand went up, so did prices. A Virginian in 1683 wrote to a slave dealer that he wanted black boys and girls of certain ages and would pay these prices:

> 3,000 lbs tobacco for every Negro boy or girl that
> shall be between the ages of seven and eleven
> years old; to give 4,000 lbs tobacco for every
> youth or girl that shall be between the ages of
> eleven to fifteen and to give 5,000 lbs tobacco for
> every young man or woman that shall be above
> fifteen years of age and not exceed twenty-four.

Sometimes "Bargains, Black and White," were advertised for sale. In the *Pennsylvania Gazette* of April 3, 1760, one such ad read: "To be sold by Thomas Overrend at the drawbridge, two white boys and a Negro lad; all about 14 years of age. Also very good lime juice, by the hogshead or gallon."

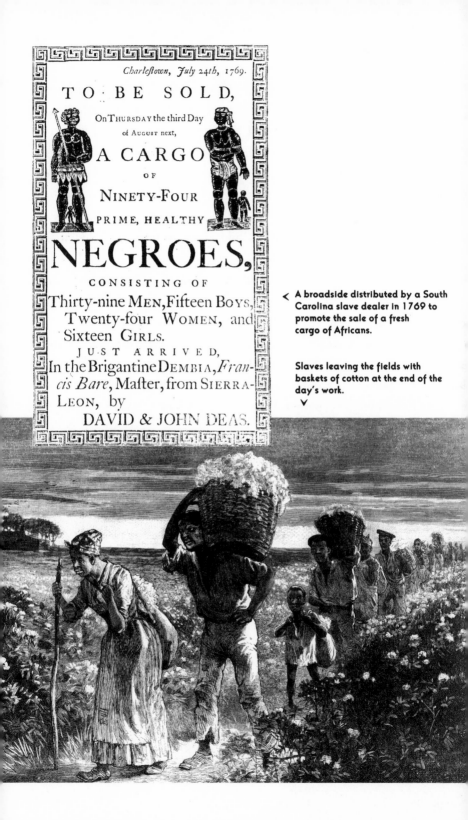

Charlestown, *July 24th,* 1769.

TO BE SOLD,

On THURSDAY the third Day
of AUGUST next,

A CARGO
OF
NINETY-FOUR
PRIME, HEALTHY
NEGROES,
CONSISTING OF
Thirty-nine MEN, Fifteen BOYS,
Twenty-four WOMEN, and
Sixteen GIRLS.
JUST ARRIVED,
In the Brigantine DEMBIA, *Fran-
cis Bare,* Master, from SIERRA-
LEON, by
DAVID & JOHN DEAS.

< A broadside distributed by a South
Carolina slave dealer in 1769 to
promote the sale of a fresh
cargo of Africans.

Slaves leaving the fields with
baskets of cotton at the end of the
day's work.
∨

Slaves—children or adults—were owned by their masters for the duration of the slave's life. The master ruled over their private lives as well as their work. Slaves were property under the law—like a horse or an acre or a house—completely at the disposal of their owners. The lives slaves lived were the lives their masters let them live.

On southern plantations, the children labored alongside the men and women. Children went into the fields at the age of five or six, or whenever the master dictated. They carried water, pulled weeds, hoed, wormed tobacco, and picked cotton. After the age of ten, they usually had the same tasks in field labor as the adults.

Girls were put to work even earlier than boys. At four or five, girls took care of babies. The evidence for this comes from the recollections of ex-slaves when they were interviewed by people from the WPA Federal Writers' Project in the 1930s:

> I was just a little small girl when Miss Earlie
> Hatchel bought me en she wouldn't let me hold
> de baby cause she was 'fraid I would drop it. I
> just sat dere on de floor en set de baby 'tween my
> legs. Father an mother belong to de old Bill
> Greggs en dat whe' Miss Earlie Hatchel buy me
> from. After dat I didn't never live wid my parents
> any more, but I went back to see dem every two
> weeks. Miss Hatchel want a nurse en dat how
> come she buys me.

A bit older, girls worked full-time in the house:

When I is about six years old they take me into
the big house to learn to be a house woman, and
they show me how to cook and clean up and take
care of babies. I didn't have to work very hard.
Just had to help the cooks and peel the potatoes
and pick the guineas and chickens and do things
like that. Sometimes I had to watch the baby. I
had to git up way before daylight and make the
fire in the kitchen fireplace and bring in some
fresh water, and go get the milk what been down
in the spring all night, and do things like that
until breakfast ready. Old Master and Old Mistress come in the big hall to eat in the summer,
and I stand behind them and shoo off the flies.

Children sold away from their master were put to work
by the new master:

When I was nine years old, dey took me from my
mother an' sol' me. Massa Tinsley made me de
house girl. I had to make de beds, clean de house
an' odder things. After I finished my reg'ler work,
I would go to de mistress' room, bow to her, an'
stand dere 'till she noticed me. Den she would
say, "Martha, is you thew wid yo' wuk?" I say
"Yes mam." She say, "No you ain'; you isn't
lowed de shades." I'd den lower de shades, fill de
water pitcher, 'range de towels on de washstand
an' anything else mistress wants me to do. Den
she'd tell me dat was 'bout all to do in dere. Den I
would go in de odder rooms in de house an' do

de same things. We wasn't 'lowed to sit down. We had to be doing something all day. Whenebber we was in de presence of any of de white folks, we had to stand up.

Regardless of the child's age, the tasks she would be ordered to do were harsh:

When I was a little bitty girl dey used to make a scarecrow outen me. Dey'd make me git up fo' daybreak an' go out into de cornfields an' set dere till way pas' dark so's to keep de crows from diggin' up de young corn that was just poppin' hits head 'bove de ground. A heap of mornin's de fros' bit my feet, an' when hit come time to go back to de cabin I could hardly walk.

Slave craftsmen, trained at an early age, did much of the skilled work on the larger plantations. James W. C. Pennington tells in his fugitive slave narrative how, at the age of eleven, he was taught the blacksmith's trade by another slave on his master's Maryland plantation. He worked at it until he was twenty-one and took great pride in his craftsmanship: "I sought to distinguish myself in the finer branches of the business by invention and finish. I frequently tried my hand at making guns and pistols, putting blades in penknives, making fancy hammers, hatchets, sword-canes, etc."

Young Pennington learned to be not only a blacksmith but a stonemason and carpenter. (Years later, as a runaway slave, he got to Europe and earned the degree of doctor of divinity at Heidelberg University in Germany. He was the first African American to write a book on the history of his people.)

Boys began with easy chores and were trained to do harder ones as they grew older. As a small boy in Baltimore, said Frederick Douglass, the most promiment black leader of the nineteenth century, "my employment was to run errands, and to take care of Tony [his master's son]; to prevent his getting in the way of carriages, and to keep him out of harm's way."

At Thomas Jefferson's Monticello in Virginia, Jefferson set up a small factory to make nails. It was worked by a dozen young slaves, ten to sixteen years old. Full of the juices of life, the boys were held to strict military discipline. They labored for twelve hours a day, six days a week. The work was so repetitive, boring, mindless, and, of course, payless that they did as little as possible. Only when an overseer or Jefferson himself was watching them were they productive. When several of the boys in his sweatshop ran off to freedom, Jefferson had them hunted down relentlessly and flogged when caught.

Slavery operated not only in the South but in the North, where it was adapted for local needs. On the farms of New York, New Jersey, and Pennsylvania, there was a heavy demand for strong slaves to help in the fields, in the household, and in the workshop. Most slave masters in the north held only a slave or two, but the large landowners owned dozens.

The little children, who often began as household servants, were put to harder work as they grew older—that is, if they reached maturity, for life expectancy was short in the colonies. Many children on southern plantations died before the age of four.

With few northern households having more than one or two slaves, it was hard for the African Americans to develop a community life. They had little contact with blacks elsewhere. Whether in the towns or on the farms, slavery separated families; children were sold away from their parents and the mother or father was usually unable to visit them. Grief at such forced breakup of the slave family was so strong that masters kept unruly slaves in line by threatening to sell the children. If a household was small and the master could not use a large work force, he would readily sell the babies of a mother who gave birth to more than he felt the household needed. So fear of separation became an abiding anxiety for the slave child.

Physical abuse, too, was an everyday threat. In New York City, for example, a seven-year-old was flogged, then forced to swallow salt so as to make him thirsty, and locked in a room with nothing to drink.

Even for taking a scrap of food, a little girl could be punished, as this account by an ex-slave shows:

> I recollects once when I was trying to clean the
> house like Old Miss tell me I finds a biscuit, hon-
> gry I et it, 'cause we never see such a thing as a
> biscuit only sometimes on Sunday morning. We
> just have corn bread and syrup and sometimes fat
> bacon, but when I et that biscuit and she comes in
> and say, "Where that biscuit?" I say, "Miss, I et it

'cause I'm so hungry." Then she grab that broom and start to beating me over the head with it and calling me low-down nigger, and I guess I just clean lost my head 'cause I knowed better than to fight her if I knowed anything 't all, but I start to fight her, and the driver, he comes in and he grabs me and starts beating me with the cat-o'-nine-tails, and he beats me till I fall to the floor nearly dead. He cut my back all to pieces, then they rubs salt in the cuts for more punishment. Lord, Lord, honey! Them was awful days.

Strict rules controlled the movements of slave children. They were not allowed out alone at night. In New York they could not go to school without the master's consent and were forbidden to meet with their friends or hunt in the woods. Even the name given a child had to be approved by the master.

"It is a pity," wrote North Carolina planter Charles Pettigrew, "that agreeable to the nature of things slavery and tyranny must go together and that there is no such thing as having an obedient and useful slave, without the painful exercise of undue and tyrannical authority."

The Cheapest Raw Material

In the time of the ancient Greeks, one of their great thinkers, Aristotle (384–322 B.C.) wrote that slavery would end someday if machines were invented to do the world's work. Then there would be no need of slaves. Two thousand years later, in the 1700s, the machine age began. But as the industrial revolution took hold, workers became enslaved to the pitiless, soulless machine. And children still worked, on factory floors vibrating with the ceaseless motion of intricate machines, and under the pressure of mill owners seeking ever greater profits.

"A totally inexperienced boy," wrote one early observer, "sets a loom with all its shuttles in motion, by simply moving a rod backwards and forwards." The new mechanical invention seemed "designed with the express purpose of

Children working alongside adults in a Lancashire, England, cotton mill, 1834.

laying the burden of the world's work upon child shoulders."

It began in eighteenth-century England. The new inventions, new technology, and new processes brought about great changes in social and economic life. England moved from a stable agricultural and commercial society to modern industrialism. (The same process soon began in other parts of Europe and in America.) Many machines were invented and sizable factories began to use them. The substitution of steam for water power allowed industry to move from the banks of streams in remote country valleys to towns, where plenty of child labor could be had. These children lived at home with their parents.

Factory towns sprang up everywhere and great fortunes were made with dizzying speed. But all this was at the cost of great poverty. By 1795 a Dr. Aikin, describing the region around Manchester, a major textile center, wrote that the best features of home life had been destroyed as filth, disease, and poverty spread everywhere. He singled out the great demand for children in the cotton mills as one of the cruelest aspects. At first parents refused to send their boys and girls into the mills. The parents were used to making goods at home, as part of domestic life, and thought factory work was degrading. But as wages were forced down when children replaced adults, hunger drove parents to send their children into the mills.

Children as young as five worked for Josiah Wedgewood, the famous maker of pottery. His chemical process was permeated with lead oxide, a deadly poison. He admitted it made the children "very subject to disease," but went right on hiring them.

In other places, too, children were employed in shocking conditions. Brickmaking is one example. Here is an eye-witness report:

> I went down to a brickfield and made a considerable inspection. I first saw, at a distance, what appeared like eight or ten pillars of clay. . . . On walking up, I found to my astonishment that these pillars were human beings. They were so like the ground on which they stood, their features were so indistinguishable, their dress so besoiled and covered with clay that, until I approached and saw them move, I believed them to be products of the earth. . . .
>
> I saw little children, three-parts naked, tottering under the weight of wet clay, some of it on their heads, and some on their shoulders, and little girls with large masses of wet, cold, and dripping clay pressing on their abdomens. Moveover, the unhappy children were exposed to the most sudden transitions of heat and cold, for, after carrying their burdens of wet clay, they had to endure the heat of the kiln, and to enter places where the heat was so intense that I was myself able to remain no more than two or three minutes.

In agriculture, too, children worked in the fields under harsh conditions. In some areas a middleman or labor broker hired out gangs of women and children to the farmers. Children of six and seven labored nine hours a day in all kinds of weather. They plodded to and from work often as much as seven miles each way. Beaten and ill-treated by the farm managers, their health was so bad that their death rate was nearly as high as in the Manchester mills.

Thousands of boys worked in Britain's coal mines. As young as seven, they were harnessed like donkeys to coal carts to haul them through the mine tunnels. A six-year-old girl could be forced to pull a load many times her own weight on fourteen long journeys daily. In 1843 it was disclosed that children as young as four were being sent down into the coal pits.

Such conditions were of little concern to the mine and mill owners. They wanted children. And they got them wholesale from the local overseers of the poor. You can get rid of your paupers, the overseers were told. It will save you money, and we'll train them for new trades. The mill owners would send their agents to pick up the children from the poorhouses and bring them to the factories packed in wagons or canal-boats. "Without remorse," wrote a lawyer in a factory district, the children were "used up as the cheapest raw material on the market." These children worked twelve, fourteen, even sixteen hours a day and often through the night. They lived in bleak factory barracks.

John Fielden, a member of the British Parliament, wrote a book titled *The Curse of the Factory System*. He gave solid evidence that thousands of children were worked to exhaustion by harsh foremen, with many beaten and starved to the point of death. Some even killed themselves rather than go on suffering. He wrote:

> In stench, in heated rooms, amid the whirring of a thousand wheels, little fingers and little feet were kept in ceaseless action, forced into unnatural activity by blows from the heavy hands and feet of the merciless overlooker, and the infliction of bodily pain by instruments of punishment invented by the sharpened ingenuity of insatiable selfishness.

In 1751 the novelist Henry Fielding, himself a British magistrate, wrote that "there are few, if any, nations or countries where the poor . . . are in a more scandalous, nasty condition than here in England."

The English historian Georgina Battiscombe describes the children's misery:

> They snatched their food as they worked, because during the official meal-breaks it fell to them to clean the machinery. Hungry and exhausted, towards the end of the day they fell asleep at their work and could only be roused by blows from the overseer's whip. They had no time for schooling, and at work they learned no skills which could be of use to them in later life. Thousands upon thousands of children were growing up with damaged, stunted bodies, and minds quite untouched by education.

Chimney sweeps in eighteenth-century England.

Not only were children in factory and coal mines treated this badly, but also the children who cleaned chimneys. "Climbing-boys," they were called. Many had been born out of wedlock in seaport towns where large numbers of prostitutes worked. Some were deserted by their parents, even sold by their parents, and others were taken from the poorhouses as young as four to do this work.

Readers of the Charles Dickens novel *Oliver Twist* will remember how the boy narrowly escaped apprenticeship to a sweep. But soon after he turned twelve, Dickens himself was put to work in a shoe-polish factory. Instead of going to school, as he had hoped, he spent long hours pasting labels onto pots of black shoe polish in a "crazy, tumble-down old house on the river literally overrun with rats." His father was broke and the family needed every penny the boy could earn.

Battiscombe tells what it was like to be a chimney sweep:

> Forced screaming and sobbing up dark, narrow chimneys, their skin scorched and lacerated, their eyes and throats filled with soot, these small chil-dren . . . faced suffocation in the blackness of a chimney or perhaps a slow and painful death from cancer of the scrotum, the climbing-boys' occupa-tional disease. Of all unhappy child-workers these were perhaps the most ill-used and forlorn.

While children in the mines and mills were not visible to the general public, the misery of the climbing-boys was plain to everyone who needed to have a chimney cleaned. Yet not until the 1870s did the law stop the practice, with machines replacing children to sweep the chimneys.

That small victory was part of the general movement to improve working conditions for children. The movement got started in the late 1700s and was given a great push forward in 1799–1800 when a deadly epidemic spread rap-idly through the Manchester factories and the surrounding countryside. Blamed for the epidemic were the factory con-ditions: overwork, poor food and clothing, bad ventilation, and overcrowding, especially among the children. Those housed in company barracks slept by turns in beds never allowed to cool, with children of both sexes and all ages herded together.

It was thanks to a group of social-minded people that the movement to protect working children got under way. They included reformers like Robert Owen, religious nonconformist; poets like Robert Southey; labor leaders; economists; and, above all, the aristocrat Lord Ashley. He was not alone among the upper-class people who were concerned with child workers. Some who were very conservative on most issues felt compassion for children. And some mill owners were among them, for not all of the owners were heartless. There were some who paid decent wages, kept their factories clean and well ventilated, provided decent cottages and gardens for their workers, built schools for the workers' children, and paid staff doctors to provide medical care. Several were members of the Society of Friends—the Quakers—who were justly famous for their concern with social problems. To make money was the object of their businesses, but they were not ruthless about it.

Lord Ashley fought the battles of the poor and oppressed in the British Parliament. It was hard going, for the dominant attitude was to let private enterprise, the "free market," take its own course without interference by government, even at the cost of vast human misery.

Still, Ashley and the other reformers managed from time to time to gain a majority in Parliament. From 1833 on, several Factory Acts were adopted that banned the employment of children under the age of nine in the textile industry, limited the hours children of various ages could work, and called for two hours of schooling a day. Other laws regulated the employment of children in field labor, prohibited apprenticing children to miners and chimney sweeps, and provided for better housing.

Ashley, who became the Earl of Shaftsbury upon his father's death, did much to lessen the extent of human misery. When he died at the age of eighty-four, working people crowded the streets of London to pay their respects to a great human being as his coffin passed on its way to burial in Westminster Abbey.

The United States would never know some of the worst evils Britain went through during its early industrial age. But child workers in America would also bear a terrible burden for all too long a time.

No Flowers Anywhere

When he was a little child, Stephen Knight began to work in a cotton mill in Rhode Island. The year was 1835. He recalls his job:

> The running time for that mill was about 14 hours per day. . . . In the summer months we went in as early as we could see. . . . From September 20 until March 20 we went to work at five o'clock in the morning and came out at eight o'clock at night. . . . For my services I was allowed 42 cents per week, which, being analyzed, was seven cents per day, or one-half cent per hour.
>
> A mother with several children suggested to the proprietor that the pay seemed small. The proprietor replied, "You get enough to keep the wolf

from the door." He then remarked, "You get enough clothes to wear, don't you?" To which she answered, "Barely enough to cover our nakedness. "Well," said the proprietor, "we want the rest."

That same year a report by the New York State Assembly stated that the 12- to 14-hour day demanded of the mill workers was "several hours more daily labor than was exacted even from the convicts in our State Prison. The children among them are necessarily brought up in a comparative ignorance, and are unfitted to become valuable citizens."

How did those children feel? What did they think about their lives? This poem, published in a magazine in 1832, tries to tell us:

> I often think how once we used in summer
>   fields to play,
> And run about and breathe the air that made us
>   glad and gay;
> We used to gather buttercups and chase the
>   butterfly;
> I loved to feel the light breeze lift my hair as it
>   went by!
>
> Do you still play in those bright fields? and are
>   the flowers still there?
> There are no fields where I live now—no
>   flowers any where!

But day by day I go and turn a dull and
    tedious wheel;
You cannot think how sad, and tired, and faint
    I often feel.

I hurry home to snatch the meal my mother can
    supply,
Then back I hasten to the task—that not to
    hate I try.
At night my mother kisses me, when she has
    combed my hair,
And laid me in my little bed, but—I'm not
    happy there:

I dream about the factory, the fines that on us
    wait—
I start and ask my father if—I have not lain
    too late?
And once I heard him sob and say—"Oh better
    were a grave,
Than such a life as this for thee, thou little
    sinless slave!"

I wonder if I ever shall obtain a holiday?
Oh, if I do, I'll go to you and spend it all in
    play!
And then I'd bring some flowers home, if you
    will give me some,
And at my work I'll think of them and
    holidays to come!

It was in the late 1790s, right after the American Revolution, that the United States' first factories began operating. A textile mill in Pawtucket, Rhode Island opened with nine workers, all of them under twelve, from poor families in the neighborhood. By the 1800s, half the nation's textile workers were under ten years of age and were working twelve or more hours a day.

What was wrong with that? asked Alexander Hamilton. He was the first secretary of the treasury and an ardent advocate of the new manufacturers. "Children," he said, "are rendered more useful by manufacturing establishments than they otherwise would be." George Washington, too, visiting a factory in Boston making canvas cloth, watched little girls at work and noted in his diary, "This is a work of public utility and private advantage."

Was putting children to work in factories any different from having them work in colonial times? Most people didn't think so. There was a universal belief in the essential goodness of work, and there was a strong fear of idleness. "The devil will find things for idle hands to do." Businessmen who built the new industries said they wouldn't be taking farmers from their essential work, since they would draw mostly on women and children. By harnessing children to machinery, the factories would increase the nation's production at low cost and would give useful jobs to the poor and the idle. So, they said, child labor was economically necessary and morally desirable.

It was Samuel Slater, the "father of American manufacturers," who developed the way to coordinate all stages of textile manufacturing from raw cotton to yarn by machinery, and who introduced children as the industrial labor force. Most of the children tended the spindles, removing and attaching bobbins. Their small, quick fingers were just right for picking up and knotting broken threads. They became, as one historian wrote, "the little fingers of the gigantic automatons of laborsaving machinery."

The factory owners were not obliged to teach the children a trade, nor provide them with a general education. In the early period, there was no legal means to prevent the abuse of young workers. Politicians backed the rise of the infant industries, but didn't think of protecting the "little fingers" that worked them.

For boys and girls in poor rural areas, the new life in the factory towns meant an escape from poverty and drudgery. They were lured away from home by dreams of an income of their own and fun with their peers in boarding-houses.

Fun? Josiah Quincy, later to be Boston's mayor and Harvard's president, took a different view. He saw children from four to ten years old operating machinery in iron, paper, and textile mills and getting 12 to 25 cents for a day's labor. The men who showed him around, he said,

> were very eloquent on the usefulness of this man-
> ufacture, and the employment it supplied to so
> many poor children. But an eloquence was ex-
> erted on the other side of the question more com-
> manding than this, which calls us to pity those
> little creatures, plying in a contracted room,
> among flyers and cogs, at an age when nature re-

A boy crippled in factory work, with his impoverished mother and her baby.

quires for them air, space and sports. There was a
dull dejection in the countenance of all of them.''

There were two systems for recruiting children to the
factories. One was the boardinghouse system, in which children—mostly young girls—worked in the factory while
their parents stayed home on the farm. The other was the
family system, used by Slater's mill and others. It brought
rural families to the mill town and housed them in tenements
built and owned by the company. The family paid rent and
bought their provisions at the company store. Everyone in
the family from about seven on up worked in the factory
from sunrise to sunset six days a week. Their only holidays
were Christmas, Easter, and half a day on the Fourth of
July.

The wages were usually so low and the cost of food at
the company store so high that the family went deeply into
debt, even though almost everyone worked. The year would
end with the family owing the mill owner more than the
total sum of their wages. Practically no one could save. The
result was an ever tighter grip by the owner upon his workers.

That early generation of child workers found it hard to
get used to the factory clock and bell time. If they tried to
quit, the owners threatened to fire the whole family. As
production speeded up, Lewis Kingman, a child in a Massachusetts mill town, hoping to slow things down, was
secretly slipping the leather belts that powered the spinning
mules off their pulley. Finally he was caught cutting them.

The owner said that "for boldness and cunning," nothing surpassed that trick. Hiram Munger recalled his experience as a child in a factory as "American slavery in the second degree."

What about the children who stayed home on the farm in this period and did not enter the factories? Remember, they were still the majority. Their chores were many, and responsible. Take Daniel Drake of Kentucky. In the early 1800s, in his childhood, he rocked the cradle of the younger children and took care of them while his mother tended to her chores. At eight, he rode on the horse to steady it while his father plowed and planted the corn seed. He spent endless hours weeding, and keeping the crows and squirrels off the young crops by tossing stones at them. At harvesting time, he bound the wheat his father had sickled and carried the sheaves. In winter, he hauled the wood his father had cut and chopped it up for the fireplace. At twelve he was plowing the field and at thirteen splitting rails, building fences, and sickling at harvest time.

Susan Blunt, a New Hampshire girl, recalled her work as a child in the 1830s. When she was about ten, her mother allowed her to keep house for a family a mile away. She had complete charge of little twin girls and an old invalid father. She got up at five, walked a long way to the well for water, then boiled potatoes, fried pork, and made coffee for breakfast. She got the twins dressed and off to school, tended to the sick father, and made dinner, including baking biscuits. For cooking, cleaning, mending, and caring for young and old, she was paid 15 cents a day. She bought a new calico apron with her earnings. Such girls, working as domestic help on a farm, were paid only one fourth to one third as much as a boy would get for farm labor.

Almost all clothing in those days was made by the very people who wore it—from producing the fabrics out of wool, linen, or flax, to cutting, fitting, and sewing the garments. "I somehow or somewhere got the idea," wrote Lucy Larcom, "when I was a small child, that the chief end of a woman was to make clothing for mankind."

To the children working in textile and other industries and to those still on the family farm, there must be added the many apprentices bound to master craftsmen. By the 1830s, under the pressure of the new industrial system, relations between master and apprentice had crumbled. The middleman bought the raw material, had the skilled parts made perhaps in his own place of business, and had the rest completed at the journeyman's shop. Competition for work intensified. Wages were cut and cheaper labor was used. Work became more and more subdivided.

Large numbers of boys and women now competed for the same job. Boys apprenticed for five, six, or seven years were taught only a part of a trade. They learned it in much less time and ran away to pick up another skill elsewhere. So easy was it to replace them with other young boys that masters hardly bothered to locate the runaways. Many offered only a penny for the return of a runaway—and that only to protect them legally from any wrong that might be done by their apprentice.

In 1830, so many journeymen printers in Philadelphia

were out of work, because boys had replaced them, that they formed a union to protect themselves. Just as in the factories, child labor was taking the place of adults in the trades.

For a long time, few people seemed to care much about child labor. Everyone was expected to work—men, women, and children—and public opinion accepted the "sunup to sundown" system of labor. Long hours were the rule everywhere. Leisure time? No one thought about that. Why shouldn't the employer ask the same hours of his workers as a farmer asked of his family, the shopkeeper gave to his trade, and the housewife devoted to her daily chores?

When a few reformers began to suggest that a ten-hour day in the factories was long enough for children to work, the mill owners argued it would have an "unhappy influence." It would interfere with their worthy attempt to get the young used to the hard work that would prepare them properly for life as adults.

This was in the 1830s, the flowering period of movements for social reforms of many kinds. Of all the grievances workers complained about, the lack of a public education system was foremost. Such schools should not be a charitable enterprise, but free and tax-supported, they urged. Yet in the 1830s, at least one million children between five and fifteen were not in school. And well over that number were illiterate. The long work hours for children sent into the factories prevented them from getting any kind of education. A labor paper in Philadelphia reported that only one of every six children in that city's mills could read and write their own names. During a strike of mill workers in Paterson, New Jersey, for an eleven-hour day, a union leaflet said of the children:

> Scarcely time allowed them to take their scanty meals, they retire to their beds at night worn down and exhausted with excessive labor—hence they are deprived of any privilege except working, eating and sleeping. Is it to be wondered at, that our country has become the great theater of mobs, yes, we may say murderers too, when we remember that the poor and their children in manufacturing towns and districts are kept in ignorance and regarded as but little superior to the beasts that perish?

A count of four thousand workers in New England's mill towns in 1832 revealed that sixteen hundred were aged seven to sixteen. No child could be taken from a mill to be placed in a school even for a short time without losing his or her job. And if parents who had a number of children in a mill withdrew one or more for schooling, the whole family was fired. The only chance such children had for schooling was either on Sundays or after eight-thirty in the evening on other days. There were a few honorable exceptions. Some mill owners provided schools for children or allowed them to attend school for about three months of the year.

It was the struggling new labor unions of the 1830s that raised the banner for a ten-hour day, and at the same time called for laws requiring children working in factories to attend school for a specified number of weeks or months each year.

Massachusetts in 1836 was the first state to adopt a compulsory school attendance law. It held that children under fifteen could be hired in manufacturing only if they had received three months of schooling in the year preceding their employment. Several states soon followed that pattern. Some went further. They banned the hiring of children under twelve in factories and established a ten-hour workday for children. These laws did not apply to children working in agriculture or in the mechanical trades.

Although only a few such laws were adopted, they were still an advance in the legal status of working children. Yet they were so poorly enforced (as such laws still are) that they did little to protect young workers. Employers found it quite easy to violate the laws without being detected or without suffering any penalty. And because parents badly needed their children's wages or were too frightened to file complaints, the mill owners got away with it. A Massachusetts inquiry reported "frequent and gross violation" of the child labor laws.

Mills, Mines, and Sweatshops

With the coming of the Civil War, America's industrial
life was transformed. Vast sums of money were spent daily
on weapons, ammunition, machinery, clothing, boots,
shoes, and canned goods. Old factories expanded and giant
new ones sprang up. Faster, better, and cheaper methods of
making products were devised.

You could see it happen in Cincinnati. The Ohio city
typified what was going on throughout the nation's manufacturing centers. After the war, a company that had made
expensive carriages for the rich began turning out cheap
mass-produced carriages for sale worldwide. Production
was subdivided into many minute and repetitive operations,
and more machinery was created to speed up each specialized
task. Soon the company was able to sell carriages at half the
price it used to charge.

What did this mean for the workers? The skilled craftsmen lost out. Women and children were hired to do the work they once performed. "In the old days," said the state labor commissioner, "before machinery supplanted the mechanic, it took a man to drive the jack plane, shape the iron and construct the vehicle; now a delicate child guiding a machine can do most of his work." So simplified did production become that young workers could be taught all they needed to know in a fraction of the time once required.

Children and women were hired at low pay in many of Cincinnati's other factories. In the furniture shops, they carried out the lighter work of painting and varnishing and preparing cane seats. In printing and publishing, they did the tedious jobs of folding, sewing, and binding. In textile mills, they ran the looms, spindles, and frames. In the shoe-making shops, they did the stitching and binding.

Children leaving home for the factory added to family income. But factory work was harmful to health and threatening to safety. Hundreds of children were packed into factory space with poor ventilation; few toilets, washrooms, or fire escapes; and little protection from dangerous machinery.

The journalist John Spargo visited the Pennsylvania and West Virginia coal mine region in the early 1900s and told in graphic detail how the boys worked in the breakers:

> Work in the coal breakers is exceedingly hard and dangerous. Crouched over the chutes, the boys sit hour after hour picking out the pieces of slate and other refuse from the coal as it rushes past to the

washers. From the cramped position they have to assume, most of them become more or less deformed and bent-backed like old men. When a boy has been working for some time and begins to get round-shouldered, his fellows say that "He's got his boy to carry round wherever he goes."

The coal is hard, and accidents to the hands, such as cut, broken, or crushed fingers, are common among the boys. Sometimes there is a worse accident: a terrified shriek is heard, and a boy is mangled and torn in the machinery, or disappears in the chute to be picked out later smothered and dead. Clouds of dust fill the breakers and are inhaled by the boys, laying the foundations for asthma and miners' consumption. . . .

I met one little fellow ten years old in Mt. Carbon, W. Va., last year, who was employed as a "trap boy." Think of what it means to be a trap boy at ten years of age. It means to sit alone in a dark mine passage hour after hour, with no human soul near; to see no living creature except the mules as they pass with their loads, or a rat or two seeking to share one's meal; to stand in water or mud that covers the ankles, chilled to the marrow by the cold draughts that rush in when you open the trap-door for the mules to pass through; to work for fourteen hours—waiting—opening and shutting a door—waiting again—for sixty cents; to reach the surface when all is wrapped in

Boys picking slate in the coal breakers of a Pennsylvania anthracite mine.

the mantle of night, and to fall to the earth ex-
hausted and have to be carried away to the nearest
"shack" to be revived before it is possible to walk
to the farther shack called "home."

A workers' newspaper, the *Labor Standard,* described the
breaker room at a Pennsylvania mine:

> In a little room in this big, black shed—a room
> not twenty feet square—forty boys are picking
> their lives away. . . .
>   These little fellows go to work in this cold
> dreary room at seven o'clock in the morning and
> work till it is too dark to see any longer. For this
> they get $1 to $3 a week. Not three boys in this
> roomful could read or write. Shut in from every-
> thing that is pleasant, with no chance to learn,
> with no knowledge of what is going on about
> them, with nothing to do but work, grinding
> their little lives away in this dusty room, they are
> no more than the wire screens that separate the
> great lumps of coal from the small. They had no
> games; when their day's work is done they are too
> tired for that. They know nothing but the differ-
> ence between slate and coal.

As in the prewar decades, boys and girls worked because
of the family's need to piece out a living. The long hours
and the grinding labor kept them from schooling, wiping
out any chance to rise above routine and low-paid labor.

You can see what the denial of schooling does to child

workers. Lawrence Fell, the chief factory inspector for New Jersey in the late 1800s, tells of his experiences with boys and girls ages ten to fifteen in the local factories:

> Nearly all the children examined were naturally bright and intelligent, but neglect, years of work and their general surroundings had left sad traces upon their youthful forms and minds. . . . There is no exaggeration in saying that three-fourths of the work-children know absolutely nothing. The greatest ignorance exists on the most common-place questions.
>
> Most of these children have never been inside a schoolhouse, and the majority have either been at school for too little a period to learn anything or have forgotten the little instruction they received. . . .
>
> The number able to read and write, in a distinguishable way, was shockingly small, and very many could neither read nor write even their own names. Very few of these children ever heard of George Washington. At least sixty percent never heard of the United States or Europe. At least thirty percent could not name the city in which they lived.

In 1870, for the first time, the federal census recorded the number of children working. They found 250,000 aged ten to fifteen in nonagricultural occupations. By 1900 these figures rose to nearly 750,000. Since the census excluded children under ten and usually missed child labor in sweatshops, domestic service, and the street trades, these figures only hint at the true extent of child labor in those years. For comparison, in the early 1880s the Children's Aid Society estimated there were at least 100,000 child workers in New York City alone. A decade later, investigators reported that 11,000 children were working in Chicago sweatshops. Pennsylvania had 120,000 children working in its mines and mills in 1900.

It was mostly immigrants who ended up in the sweatshops. Around 1880 the exodus of millions from Eastern and Southern Europe began. About four million were driven from Russia and Poland, many by pogroms, the mass killing of Jews by anti-Semitic mobs encouraged and even organized by the authorities. Jews suffered less violent forms of persecution as well. An ever-growing body of restrictive laws penned Jews up in huge ghettos. Quotas barred all but a few from schools and universities. They had little choice in where they could live or in how they could earn a living. They looked to America for asylum. This was the land of opportunity, they believed, where they could live in freedom and work their way up to realize their own possibilities.

One of those who fled Russia was David Edelstadt, a childhood witness of the Kiev pogrom of 1881. At sixteen he reached America and went to work for three long years in Cincinnati making buttonholes in a garment factory. He wrote passionate poems of protest against sweatshop conditions that were set to music and sung by Jewish workers everywhere. At twenty-six, stricken with tuberculosis, the sweatshop disease, he died.

Nationwide in 1910, the number of children earning

wages outside the home reached two million—almost half of them girls. Two out of five held jobs where conditions were the worst and employers the most ruthless—in mines, factories, textile mills, and tenement workshops. In the clothing industry, their wages averaged $2 a week. In glass and textile industries, it was less than $3 a week.

The sweatshops of this era employed many immigrants from Italy as well as Eastern Europe. Every one of those new arrivals had to work: young, old, sick or well, toddlers or teenagers. They strung beads, sewed buttons, plucked feathers, twisted paper and wires into artificial flowers. And they did this for minimal pay—5 or 6 cents an hour was a common wage. In those small, cramped rooms there was often no air, no heat, no windows, no hot water. Lint, dust, dirt, and bits and pieces of the materials they worked with permeated the rooms, the food, the water, the beds. Filth was inevitable; the sweatshops were breeding grounds for tuberculosis and other diseases of the poor. Whole families labored twelve and fourteen hours a day, yet earned so little they lived on the edge of starvation. A journalist who managed to get into a Chicago sweatshop interviewed the children. One little girl, Ida, told him she was eleven and worked from seven A.M. to nine P.M. for $1 a week. She had been in America three years and had started to work at nine. She got 10 cents a dozen for making knee pants.

Child labor that was so terribly exploited caused one Chicago labor editor to explode:

When Jesus said, "Suffer little children to come unto me," He did not have a shirt or cloak fac-

tory, nor a planing mill that He wanted to put
them into at 40 cents a day. He wanted to bless
them and show them the light.

Not long after, a popular American poet, Ella Wheeler
Wilcox, wrote these lines against child labor:

> *In this boasted land of freedom there are bonded*
> *   baby slaves,*
> *And the busy world goes by and does not heed.*
> *They are driven to the mill, just to glut and*
> *   overfill*
> *Bursting coffers of the mighty monarch, Greed.*
> *When they perish we are told it is God's will.*
> *Oh, the roaring of the mill, of the mill!*

Watching the new immigrants who could find work only
in sweatshops, the poet Edwin Markham described what
he saw in *Cosmopolitan* magazine:

> In unaired rooms, mothers and fathers sew by day
> and by night. Those in the home sweatshop must
> work cheaper than those in the factory sweat-
> shops. And the children are called in from play to
> drive and drudge beside their elders. . . .
>
>   Is it not a cruel civilization that allows little
> hearts and little shoulders to strain under these
> grown-up responsibilities, while in the same city,
> a pet cur is jewelled and pampered and aired on a
> fine lady's velvet lap on the beautiful boulevards?

In the days before mass production of tobacco products, many children made cigarettes in the home. Most were paid nothing while learning the trade, and in some cases they paid tuition for the privilege. Lucy Lang, at the age of ten, worked in a cigar-making shop in Chicago. Her hours were seven A.M. to six P.M. for $1 a week. Because carfare would have eaten up her pay, she walked to work, an hour each way. Young Sam Cohen put in just as many hours in a cigarette factory in New York. The tobacco stuck in his nose and throat, and it was intricate and difficult work. But by the second week on the job, he was able to make four thousand cigarettes, at 80 cents per thousand, minus shortages and poor work, and received $3.10 in his pay envelope. "I could almost eat for that," he said.

Street trades drew a great number of immigrant children. At eight, William Zorach (later a noted sculptor) began selling papers and shining shoes on the streets of Cleveland. At twelve he tried for better jobs, answering the "Boy Wanted" notices. But what he found, nobody else wanted:

> The jobs never lasted more than a few days or a week. . . . I got a machine shop job; a boy told me, "Watch yourself. The last kid working that punch machine lost all his fingers on one hand." I stuck a bar into the machine and broke it. I was fired. I had a job in a hat factory and got bored to death dusting hats. There was a job in a brass factory working with buffing wheels in an atmosphere dense with metal dust, which filled the

Young workers in a glass factory.

Making hats.

lungs and eyes and left one coated from head to
foot with brass. My job was to dip the hot brass
in benzine and roll it in sawdust. It was so painful
to the hands that I was in agony. I quit.

Such conditions of work were ruinous to the health of
children. Florence Kelley, a reformer who lived in Chicago's
Hull House settlement, became chief factory inspector for
Illinois. She exposed what factory labor did to children:

It is a lamentable fact . . . that children are found
in greater number where the conditions of labor
are most dangerous to life and health. Among the
occupations in which children are employed in
Chicago, and which most endanger the health,
are: the tobacco trade, nicotine poisoning finding
as many victims among factory children as among
the boys who are voluntary devotees of the weed,
consumers of the daily cigarette included; frame
gilding, in which work a child's fingers are stiff-
ened and throat disease is contracted; button-hol-
ing, machine stitching and hand-work in tailor or
sweat shops, the machine work producing spinal
curvature, and for girls pelvic disorders also,
while the unsanitary condition of the shops makes
even hand-sewing dangerous; bakeries, where
children slowly roast before the ovens; binderies,
paper-box and paint factories, where arsenical
paper, rotting paste, and the poison of the paints
are injurious; boiler-plate works, cutlery works,

and metal-stamping works, where the dust produces lung disease; the handling of hot metal, accidents; the hammering of plate, deafness. In addition to the diseases incidental to trades, there are the conditions of bad sanitation and long hours, almost universal in the factories where children are employed.

Who was to blame for the children in bondage? Did poor families have any choice? At the wages a father worked for, he could not afford to send his children to school. Women and children had to work to keep the household going. The whole family was sacrificed to the drive of the business world for the greatest profit.

But what seemed to be a solution for individual families actually prolonged their poverty. Back in 1888, Samuel Gompers, the labor leader, tried to make workers see that:

Some of you may be tempted to send your children out to work. That may seem a very grateful addition to the income. But don't you know that the child is employed because its labor can be had cheaper than that of a man? He becomes a competitor of his father. And if the father is not discharged, some other child's father often is. In this competition, the rates of labor are often so reduced that the combined wages of the father and child are less than the father's wages alone before. . . . It is bad even from an economic point of view to send young children out to work.

That is no less true today. Frances Tan, a labor analyst in Hong Kong, recently pointed out that "in most Asian countries, cheap child workers take jobs from adults, and since they do not have the chance to develop their talents in school, they will have little, besides their unskilled labor, to contribute to the economy when they become adults."

The Most Beautiful Sight Is the Child at Labor

"In the sweatshops . . . the kindergartens are robbed to provide baby slaves," wrote John Spargo in 1906.

Unbelievable? Infants of three, four, and five working?

But that is what investigators like Spargo found to be terribly true well into the twentieth century. The little kids sat with their families and shared in the work. They wrapped paper around pieces of wire, they sorted beads, they pulled basting threads, they arranged the petals of artificial flowers, they pasted boxes for candy, they made wigs of human hair, they made lampshades.

In 1902, the young Eleanor Roosevelt, niece of President Theodore Roosevelt, helped the Consumers' League to investigate sweatshops:

> I was 18 years old when I first went with the Consumers' League into sweatshops in New York City. For the first time in my life I saw conditions I would not have believed existed, women and children working in dark, crowded quarters, toiling, I was told, all day long and way into the night to earn a few pennies. I can never forget these conditions.

The textile mills ranked first in what journalists called the "enslavement" of children in that era. Many as young as five, six, or seven worked a twelve-hour shift, by night as well as by day.

In the South, the mill-hand families usually moved directly from farm to factory. They lived in company-owned shacks, loosely built, weather-stained houses with no porch or even doorstep, lined along a dusty road. Inside, a caved-in bed or two, a few broken chairs, a rickety table, and a jumble of battered crockery.

The company store advanced supplies against wages. Everything in the company town was owned by the mill corporation, including school and church, with teacher and preacher paid and controlled by the company.

The wages in the mills were miserably low, so the children had to work. Around 1900, children of ten to fifteen made up a fourth of the labor force. They worked the same hours as their parents—as many as seventy hours per week—and for 10 or 12 cents a day.

Yet the corporations prided themselves on their paternalism. "We take care of our own," said Asa G. Candler, a major Atlanta investor. "The most beautiful sight that we see is the child at labor; as early as he may get at labor the more beautiful, the more useful does his life get to be."

Beautiful to see a ten-year-old child leave at dawn for the mill and return home long after dark? Visitors to the South noticed the teenage factory girls with "dull heavy eye, yellow, blotched complexion, dead-looking hair." By thirty, they were "wrinkled, bent and haggard"—and as illiterate as when they started out in life.

Were the northern textile mills any better? At least in one respect: they were hiring fewer and fewer children under sixteen around the turn of the century, while in the South children continued to be 25 percent of the working force. One evening, the reporter John Spargo stood outside a large flax mill in Paterson, New Jersey, and watched the crowd of men, women, and children as they left work. He talked with Marie, a little girl who said she was thirteen but was smaller than most children of ten. He wrote:

> If my little Paterson friend was 13, perhaps the nature of her employment will explain her puny, stunted body. She worked in the "steaming room" of the flax mill. All day long, in a room filled with clouds of steam, she has to stand barefooted in pools of water twisting coils of wet hemp. When I saw her she was dripping wet, though she said she had worn a rubber apron all day. In the coldest evenings of winter, little Marie, and hundreds of other little girls, must go out

from the superheated steaming rooms into the bitter cold in just that condition. No wonder that
such children are stunted and underdeveloped.

The biggest textile town in the world was Lawrence,
Massachusetts. Founded in 1845 as a "model" industrial
enterprise, by 1912 it led the nation in the production of
woolen worsteds. Two thirds of Lawrence's population of
eighty-five thousand depended on the textile mill payrolls.
Immigrants of thirty different nationalities worked in its
mills.

One half of the labor force were women and children.
The top wage for workers—usually heads of families—was
about $8 a week, or some $400 a year. No one could support
a family on that, even by living in the meanest way. So one
after another, the rest of the family had to go into the mills—
wife first, then the children, as fast as they reached the legal
age of fourteen. (Many parents falsified their children's ages
and sent them to work at an even earlier age.) At fourteen,
the typical immigrant boy or girl would leave school, no
matter how good his or her grades, and spend ten hours a
day in the mills.

The families lived in four-story wooden tenements
jammed so close together that fires, vermin, and filth took
a heavy toll on life and health. Workers came close to the
starving point. In a city that produced abundant cloth, thousands went poorly dressed. The death rate from malnutrition, exposure, and poor sanitary conditions was the highest
in the nation. Young children died at an appalling rate.

Refusing to take it any longer, the textile workers rebelled in January 1912. Organized into a union by the Industrial Workers of the World (IWW), they struck for better wages, and after workers spent a bitter ten weeks on the winter picket line, the mill owners gave in to all their demands. Wages throughout the New England textile industry were raised from 5 to 20 percent. It was great victory for human solidarity. But a striker who got a 10 percent increase in a 6- or 7-dollar-a-week pay envelope was still forced to live far below a civilized standard. What did 60 or 70 cents more a week really mean in bread, in rent, in clothing, and in fuel for a family of children?

But whatever their future, the men, women, and children of Lawrence had realized their own value and dignity as they fought for their rights.

In the southern textile mills, the wages of the workers were lower than in the North, and the working hours were longer. An eyewitness account of how children five, six, and seven years of age worked amid the looms of South Carolina's cotton mills comes from Marie Van Vorst, one of the early investigators of child labor:

> Through the looms I catch sight of Upton's, my landlord's, little child. She is seven; so small that they have a box for her to stand upon. She is a pretty, frail, little thing, a spooler—"a good spooler, tew!" Through the frames on the other side I can only see her fingers as they clutch at the flying spools; her head is not high enough, even with the box, to be visible. Her hands are fairy hands, fine-boned, well-made, only they are so

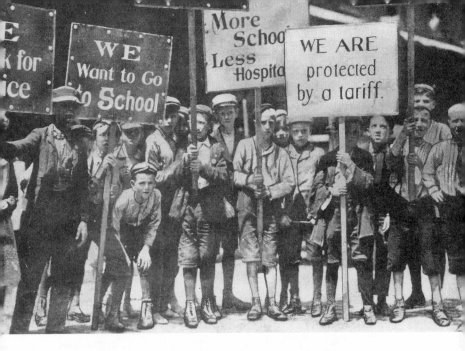

Young textile workers striking in Philadelphia at the turn of the century.

A child worker in a southern textile mill.

thin and dirty, and nails—claws: she would do well to have them cut. A nail can be torn from the finger, is torn from the finger frequently, by this flying spool. I go over to Upton's little girl. Her spindles are not thinner nor her spools whiter.

"How old are you?"

"Ten."

She looks six. It is impossible to know if what she says is true. The children are commanded both by parents and bosses to advance their ages when asked.

"Tired?"

She nods, without stopping. She is a "remarkable fine hand." She makes 40 cents a day. See the value of this labor to the manufacturer—cheap, yet skilled; to the parent it represents $2.40 per week. . . .

Here is a slender little boy—a birch rod (good old simile) is not more slender, but the birch has the advantage: it is elastic—it bends, has youth in it. This boy looks ninety. He is a dwarf; twelve years old, he appears seven, no more. He sweeps the cotton off the floor of "the baby mill." (How tenderly and proudly the owners speak of their brick and mortar.) He sweeps the cotton and lint from the mill aisles from 6 P.M. to 6 A.M. without a break in the night's routine. He stops of his own accord, however, to cough and expectorate—he has advanced tuberculosis.

At night the shanties receive us. On a pine

board is spread our food—can you call it nourish-
ment? The hominy and molasses is the best part;
salt pork and ham are strong victuals.

It is eight o'clock when the children reach their
homes—later if the mill work is behind-hand and
they are kept over hours. They are usually beyond
speech. They fall asleep at the table, on the stairs;
they are carried to bed and there laid down as
they are, unwashed, undressed; and the inanimate
bundles of rags so lie until the mill summons
them with its imperious cry before sunrise, while
they are still in stupid sleep.

Later, during the Great Depression of the 1930s, American
industry was crippled by the economic crisis. Some factories
shut down altogether, some laid off workers, and most cut
wages, lengthened hours, and speeded up their machines.
By 1933, sixteen million people had lost their jobs.

Two professors, Katherine Lumpkin and Dorothy Douglas,
made a field study of what was happening to child workers
in America. A girl they talked with, hurt badly by a car,
had to quit school at twelve and find work to help her poor
family. But without training she could get only the dullest
and most poorly paid jobs. At fourteen, she wound up in
a knitting factory as a seamer. Here is her story:

This is my daily program.
At 5:30 it is time for me to get up. I am tired
and sleepy. After I get up, I hurriedly eat my
breakfast, and I am ready to go to work. It is a
chilly winter morning, but I know that it will be

hot in the mill. I start on my three-mile walk to the factory. As I walk, I see others hurrying to work. I look at the older people and wonder if they, too, feel the resentment every morning that I do, or if as the years go by their spirits are deadened.

I arrive at the factory. The sight that I dread to see meets my eyes: the line of unemployed people waiting for the boss to come and hoping for work.

As I open the door, a force of hot stuffy air greets me. I rush to my machine, as all the girls do, to get ready, so that when the whistle blows we can start working. When doing piece work, every minute counts.

I seam men's heavy underwear. After I finish twelve union suits, I get a check for 6 cents for size fifty, and 4½ cents for the smaller sizes. At the end of the week, I paste my checks in a book and give the book to the boss, who pays according to the number of checks I have. After I finish a dozen union suits, I tie them up and carry them to the bin. The dozens are heavy, and grow heavier as the day goes on. The bin is usually full, and as I throw my dozen up on the top it very often comes down on me. Of course I fall. Rupture is quite common from carrying the heavy dozens.

Nothing much has happened today. My machine has broken twice, and because the machinist has not been very busy, I have had to wait only about three-quarters of an hour. After my many trips to the bin for my work, and after finishing each dozen, tying it up, signing my number on the check, then carrying it to the next bin, I am so tired that my body and mind grow numb. To arouse myself, I go to the ladies' room. The toilet does not flush very well, but it never does anyway. When I come to the water fountain, no matter how tired and numb I may feel, I am always angry and disgusted. That water is lukewarm; the fountain is rusty and filthy. But my trip to the fountain serves as a stimulant because I am always glad to get back to my bench.

As usual, half of my lunch has been spoiled. I can either put it on the table where I keep my work and where it becomes squashed, or I can put it in a box under my bench and give the rats the first choice.

After a monotonous afternoon, it is almost time to go home. We have three minutes to put our coats on; then we wait in our respective aisles. All eyes are on the boss, waiting for the signal. Then we rush out. This race track scene is part of the working day. When I come out, a force of fresh air meets me, the air that I have been longing for all day. My subconscious mind is aware of this, but I am so tired that I only feel my aching bones and my tired eyes.

More than two and a half million boys and girls under eighteen were working in the 1930s. A fourth of them were ten to fifteen. And tens of thousands who worked in street trades, home sweatshops, or on the farm were under ten. In many places, the children themselves were not paid a wage. Their parents were hired to do as much work with their family's labor as they could manage. The children's work was simply made a precondition to hiring the parent.

Mary, an eight-year-old, worked in Newark, New Jersey, with her mother, four brothers and sisters, and her grandma, making doll clothes. (Her father, unemployed, was often away looking for work.) The piece rates were terribly low. To meet the contractor's demands, her mother had each child do one of four different processes that their small hands could manage—cutting threads, clipping apart the trimming from one dress to the next (her mother stitched them on the machine in batches to save time), turning the finished garments right side out, and packing them in a box. It was boring, tiring; sometimes they thought they'd go crazy.

The kinds of jobs children took seem endless. Boys of ten sold newspapers on city streets, earning 5 to 9 cents per hour, and working after school until nine or even twelve at night. The average child put in eighteen hours a week and earned 82 cents. Many newsboys, some as young as six, worked illegally.

Tens of thousands of young girls worked in domestic service. The jobs offered such wretched pay and working conditions that adults shied away. Children did housework for from fifty to seventy hours a week, their pay ranging from $1 a week to $5.

There were child labor laws in some states regulating what kinds of work children might do. But canneries were usually

A newsboy asleep on a stairway.

A tenement sweatshop showing a whole family working together.

exempt because of pressure on legislatures in the major canning states. Take Mississippi, where oyster and shrimp canning was done all through the winter months. Children could shuck oysters as well as adults. Since they were paid by their output, it didn't matter much if they were slower. Shrimp had to be worked on ice. The child picked up the icy shrimp, broke off the head with one hand, and squeezed out the meat into a cup with the other. They also "cleaned" the shrimp: after it was washed, boiled, and cooled, they went through to pick out bits of shell that might have stuck.

Even lumber mills, especially in the South, employed children. At logging, boys as young as thirteen and fourteen were hired along with their fathers, doing work known to loggers as backbreaking and fit only for men.

In wood-working factories, children made crates for strawberries, baskets for vegetables, and barrels for potatoes. They ordinarily worked a ten-hour day, but twelve or more in rush seasons. Wages were very low. The boys helped, too, on the stapling machines, which, without a protective device could do great harm, even to skilled operators. Yet in many places investigators found machines without guards.

It's hard to describe in detail the places where you'd find child labor in the era of the 1930s. To give you a graphic idea of the surprising number and variety of operations that used children—in industry, agriculture, and trade—here is a partial list, drawn from a 1930s study of child labor, of the tasks boys and girls were called on to do:

COTTON TEXTILE MILLS: quill boy, battery girl, helper in weave room, clerk, doffer, sweeper, spinner, spare hand spinner, bobbin boy, office boy, buttonholer, marks roving, spooler, spare hand in weave room, assistant cloth inspector.

FOOD FACTORIES: apprentice, grader (pickles), bottler (pickles), pitting dates, packing, weighing, general helper.

CANDY FACTORIES: packing, wrapper, floor girl.

PAPER MILLS: sorting waste or rags, machine tender, hand work, edger, cut and tie tapes, packer.

SHOE FACTORIES: helper (cobbler's shop), "hand work" or "table work," lacing shoes, general helper, cementing.

FOUNDRY: cleaning molded parts, helper to crane operator, coremaking.

MACHINE SHOP: helper.

COSMETICS FACTORIES: labeling perfumes, putting stoppers in bottles, filling bottles.

LABORATORY SUPPLIES AND CHEMICALS: assembling, packing bottles.

LUMBER: pole peeling, logging.

PAPER BOX FACTORIES: turning in, lidding up, bending, covering, shaping, packing, gluing off, wrapping.

STREET TRADES: selling newspapers, delivering newspapers, shoeshining, peddling.

INDUSTRIAL HOMEWORK: children help in work on men's, women's and children's clothing, neckwear, artificial flowers, feathers, trimming novelties, stationery, lamp shades, jewelry, lace, dolls, toys, folding and pasting cellophane envelopes, sorting waste and rags (sometimes before they are washed).

CLERICAL WORK: unskilled, in stores, banks, telephone and telegraph companies, offices of factories, and other offices of all sorts and kinds. Occasionally bill clerks, helpers in shipping departments, filers, book-keepers, etc.

GROCERY STORES: delivery boy and clerk, driver of delivery wagon, selling clerk.

BAKERIES RETAIL: baker's helper, general helper, delivery boy, helper sales.

MEAT AND FISH MARKETS: bundle boy, fish cutter, butcher's helper.

COMMUNICATIONS AND TRADE: helper on wagon for junk dealer; messenger for taxi company; laborer, hauling on truck; messenger for printing company; messenger for telegraph company; helper on milkman's truck; helper on moving company truck.

LABORERS: in manufacturing industries. (In 1930 many boys and girls of 14 and 15, and a few under 14, were listed as "laborers" in all the different industries.)

DOMESTIC SERVICE: mother's helper, housework.

LAUNDRIES: folder, shaker, wrapper.

TEA-ROOMS, RESTAURANTS, ETC.: curb boy, waitress, preparing fruits, cashier, selling clerk.

HOTELS: bellboy.

OTHER PERSONAL SERVICE: kitchen helper in clinic; hospital-waitress, seamstress, cleaning; apprentice in beauty parlor; apprentice in barbershop; usher in movie

theater; general helper in pottery works; auto polisher
in garage; printing machine worker.

CANNERIES: can boys, can girls, peeling tomatoes, snip-
ping beans, shucking and cleaning corn, inspecting vegetables and berries on tables or at moving belts,
"shucking" oysters, "peeling" or "picking" shrimp,
and other processes of a miscellaneous kind.

GRAIN REGIONS: hoeing, picking up potatoes, picking
and husking corn, shocking grain, hauling of all kinds;
herding cattle, helping to butcher, cleaning seeds, clear-
ing fields of stones and thistles, preparing manure for
fuel, helping with sheep shearing, plowing.

CRANBERRY BOGS: picking.

Didn't anyone care? Didn't anyone try to protect child
workers from long hours, low pay, harsh conditions, and
dangerous work? From losing out on time to play? On
education? On their future?

Did Anyone Care?

Yes, there were people who cared about the evils of child labor. Unions, women's clubs, educators, and the Democratic party pushed for tougher labor laws. In 1904 the reformers got together and formed the National Child Labor Committee. It sent investigators around the country to report on the condition of young workers. Employers the investigators talked to often excused child labor with the same argument. Felix Adler, the head of NCLC, answered them:

> A manufacturer, standing near the furnace of a
> glass-house and pointing to a procession of young
> Slav boys who were carrying the glass on trays
> remarked: "Look at their faces, and you will see
> that it is idle to take them from the glass-house in

order to give them an education; they are what
they are, and will always remain what they are."
He meant that there are some human beings who
are mentally irredeemable, so fast asleep intellec-
tually that they cannot be awakened; designed by
nature, therefore, to be hewers of wood and
drawers of water. This cruel and wicked thing
was said of Slavs; it is the same thing which has
been said from time immemorial by the slave
owners of their slaves. First they degrade human
beings by denying them the opportunity to develop their better nature; no school, no teaching,
no freedom, no outlook; and then, as if in mock-
ery, they point to the degraded condition of their
victims as a reason why they should never be allowed to escape from it.

The reform movement found new allies when a group of
journalists called the "muckrakers" began to expose many
things wrong with American society. They named names
and places. They made their own investigations of corrup-
tion, of inequality, of injustice, of racism. Hundreds of
muckraking articles and many books appeared in the early
1900s. They reawakened the country's conscience.

Soon there were so many activists, they became a movement called the Progressives. No, they had no blueprint for
a better society. They differed from one another in many
ways. But all wished to see the promise of American life
fulfilled for the great mass of Americans.

In 1911, a terrible tragedy outraged the public and spurred

the drive for laws to protect working men, women, and children. More than 140 young women—many of them teenagers—died when a fire broke out in the Triangle Shirtwaist Factory on the upper floors of a building in New York City. Some of the victims were burned to death, others were overcome by smoke, and many died jumping from windows in a desperate effort to escape the flames. Investigations revealed shocking conditions in the building, ignored by management.

The day after the Triangle fire, Rabbi Stephen Wise, an activist for human rights, spoke these words:

> We have laws that in a crisis we find are no laws and we have enforcement that when the hour of trial comes we find is no enforcement. Let us lift up the industrial standards until they will bear inspection. And when we go before the legislators let us not allow them to cut us off with the old answer, "We have no money."

The Triangle disaster began a revolution in laws for the protection of workers in factories. The next year, 1912, Theodore Roosevelt, running on the Progressive party ticket for president, called for a federal law doing away with child labor. He lost, but the Triangle tragedy led New York State to adopt several factory laws. Urged on by Progressives, by 1914 every state but one had a minimum working age of at least twelve. However, the laws varied widely and were full of loopholes. Plainly, they weren't doing the job.

Reformers turned to the federal government for help. The

Identifying young women who died in the Triangle Shirtwaist Company fire of 1911.

A view of the burned-out factory floor in the Triangle Building.

employers fought them. They liked being able to move factories in high-wage states to low-wage states. They could play off one state against another. You couldn't do that under a federal law.

All right, said the backers of child labor protection. Then let's get a federal law passed, making regulations uniform nationwide. After all, European governments had long ago passed national laws to limit child labor. However, it wasn't easy to do that in America. The United States Constitution limits federal intervention in the business of the states. But it does give Congress the right to control trade between the states. Hammered at by the reformers, Congress passed the Child Labor Act in 1916. It banned interstate commerce in products made by children under sixteen in mines and under fourteen in factories. This was a big first: the United States had decided to protect America's working children.

It was a brief victory. Employers cried out that the government had gone beyond the lawful limits. And in 1918, the U.S. Supreme Court agreed—narrowly, by a five-to-four decision. It tossed out the Child Labor Act as unconstitutional. Again, in 1919, another federal child labor law was adopted. The employers got the court to kill that one, too, in 1922.

But during the brief period that the federal laws were operating, so much progress was made that reformers decided to try to overcome the court's rulings. They got Congress to pass a constitutional amendment in 1924. It authorized federal law for regulating the labor of persons under eighteen. Immediately the manufacturers attacked it as "socialistic" and the media echoed them. While the amendment was ratified by a majority of the states, it failed to gain the required three-fourths of all the states.

Not until 1938 did a federal law pass that set standards for child labor. It happened during President Franklin D. Roosevelt's second term in the White House. Congress had adopted a flood of new laws called the New Deal early in FDR's first term—mostly measures to fight the Great Depression. The hungry poor were given federal relief. The unemployed were put to work on many kinds of government projects that greatly enriched the nation's life. The Civilian Conservation Corps put unemployed young men from poor families at work on various conservation projects. An organization called the National Youth Administration helped students get through college by paying for work they did in their schools.

The New Deal proved to be very popular, even though the legislation did not end the Depression. Unemployment stayed very high.

FDR feared much of his New Deal would be declared unconstitutional by the conservative Supreme Court, for the new laws increased the power of the federal government. But when those justices who opposed the New Deal died or retired, he appointed justices favorable to his program in their place.

In 1938, more New Deal laws were passed. One of the most important and enduring was the Fair Labor Standards Act. It set the length of a normal work week at forty hours and established a national minimum wage. And it promoted child labor reform by setting a basic standard for the employment of young people. Boys and girls sixteen and over could be employed in most occupations, except those the U.S. secretary of labor declared to be oppressive or hazardous or harmful to their health or well-being. The minimum age for such occupations was set at eighteen. Young people fourteen and fifteen were allowed to work in only a limited number of occupations and only outside school hours. In field harvest work, under narrowly prescribed conditions, children as young as ten may be employed with the permission of the Department of Labor. Child labor laws were at last declared constitutionally legal.

All fifty states (the District of Columbia and Puerto Rico, too) now have child labor laws that regulate the employment of children who are not involved in interstate commerce. In most state laws, there is a minimum age for general work, a higher age for hazardous work, and limits on the daily and weekly hours of work. There are many differences between the federal and state child labor laws. In cases where both apply, the higher standard must be observed.

So a hundred years after the first state laws of the 1830s, the laboring conditions of children seemed no longer to be an issue. Now more than fifty years have passed since the Fair Labor Standards measure became law. Child labor, then, should be something like smallpox—a plague of the past that has largely been wiped out.

But has it been?

Fast Food—High Abuse

Operation Child Watch, it was called. For three days in 1990, five hundred inspectors from the U.S. Department of Labor swept through thirty-four hundred garment factories, fast food outlets, supermarkets, movie theaters, and hotels in search of kids working too young, too long, and too hard.

They uncovered seven thousand children who were illegally employed, and breaches of other regulations in almost half the targeted businesses—all told, eleven thousand violations of the federal labor laws. The dramatic exposure made front-page stories everywhere. Now the country knew that child labor abuses were not a thing of the past.

That was 1990. The year before, twenty-three thousand violations were reported to the Department of Labor. It was double the number reported in earlier years of that decade. It showed that employers were turning more and more to

An underage garment worker on the job during school hours is interviewed by a United States government investigator.

kids to fill menial jobs at low wages. And remember, these numbers cover only complaints made to official agencies. Experts reason that far more violations occur than are ever reported.

Just how many children are at work now? No one has an exact count. But federal sources hold that at least four million children ages fourteen to eighteen are legally employed. Another two million work illegally. Among this last group are children employed in businesses that pay them in cash to avoid taxes and the minimum wage. Or, more harmfully, children who work too many hours, late hours, at dangerous jobs, or who are under the minimum age of fourteen and therefore are too young to work at all, except on farms.

A report by the General Accounting Office, the investigating arm of Congress, held that the number of illegally employed young people almost tripled between 1983 and 1991. And a study of the 1988 census data showed that at least 166,000 fifteen-year-olds were working too many hours or in jobs that are prohibited for children that young. More than half were employed in banned occupations.

While no one would defend these violations of the laws, everyone agrees there is a positive side to children working. Parents, vocational counselors, employers, and the kids themselves believe in the benefits of work. A job can develop a sense of responsibility, discipline, teamwork. It bridges the transition from childhood to maturity. Boys and girls can master new skills and learn to organize their time. If you experience a variety of jobs while young it may shape your choice of how to make a living in the future. A good employer or supervisor can be someone to learn from—a mentor. And finally, a job well done strengthens your confidence and pride.

As for your earnings, they provide money that can be used for college savings or to help support your family. Or for travel, or personal extras you couldn't otherwise obtain.

But what explains the growth of both legal and illegal child labor in recent times? Dr. Philip J. Landrigan, chairman of the Department of Community Medicine at Mount Sinai Medical Center in New York lists these factors:

1. More and more families slid into poverty in the 1980s and the early 1990s, and that trend continues. They need the money from their children's work. It's reported that

the population will decline, leading to a shortage of adult workers. That will push employers to hire more children in the years ahead.

2. Unstable world conditions, particularly war and poverty, have led growing number of immigrants, legal and illegal, to pour into America. Often they come from countries where child labor is common. Their great need for income and their fear of discovery by immigration officials provides a huge number of people ripe for exploitation.

3. State and federal governments have cut their budgets for inspecting the workplaces. It makes the discovery of violations—and their elimination—less likely.

In chapter 7, we listed some of the huge variety of jobs children worked at in the 1930s—before the passage of the 1938 Fair Labor Standards Act. Some of those occupations no longer exist and others are prohibited to children. But many children can still be found in a number of them. Not long ago, the question arose of employing kids as batboys or batgirls by professional baseball teams. Some children as young as nine to thirteen were working in ball parks from three-thirty P.M. to as late as midnight. They were paid about $4 per game—about six working hours on average. Many worked later than nine P.M. on school nights. Some people argue that children under sixteen in such late-night jobs could be physically harmed, could fail to do their schoolwork, and are really being exploited. But others reply that a job as batboy or batgirl is more fun than work, an honor for the kids chosen, and encourages good health and character. The issue is still "under study" by the Congress, with no action taken.

Another issue is door-to-door sales by young children. Companies hire kids to peddle anything from magazine subscriptions to chemical cleaners. The hiring agents may be honorable, or they may not be. A Department of Labor study found that some companies forced the young workers to pay kickbacks, gave them late-night assignments, abused them, molested them, and placed them in high-risk environments. When *The Washington Post* investigated door-to-door candy sales, it reported that most of the child sales force "are poor, come from single-parent families, and have spent time in emergency shelters. The people who employ them say selling teaches them self-respect and business skills." But the *Post* added that "advocates for the disadvantaged, leery of the adults who run these operations, say their existence points to a deeper problem."

How illegal door-to-door sales operate was described by Patrick Mayo, a police officer in Fresno, California, in testimony before the Employment and Housing Subcommittee of Congress, chaired by Tom Lantos:

> The way the scam works is individuals put together a little team. They will then put out flyers on telephone poles near high schools or junior high schools telling these juveniles to contact them and that there is free work. Then, what they will do is they will contact a candy company or some knickknack company, and in this particular case, they will buy a box of candy for about a $1.50

and get 10 children from schools to sell the candy for $5 a box. The way they scam the citizens is that this particular organization was called "Young Minds at Work," and they present a little portfolio and they give a speech at each door, and they make the citizens feel that by giving the $5 to buy the candy, they are helping these children stay off the street, they are gainfully employed, there are activities for the children and everything else.

The bottom line is it is a scam. The child labor violations in this case were . . . too many hours, the kids were not studying for school at all, they were driving around in an uninsured motor vehicle, they were not wearing seat belts, they were not being checked on every, I believe, 2 hours or so—20 minutes? OK. 20 minutes. They were not being checked on every 20 minutes.

Talking to the children that I interviewed, several of them had been mugged by neighborhood kids for their money and everything else. They were being kicked back $2 for every $5 box of candy that they sold. They were not receiving minimum wage as per the law. They were working on an average 6 hours per night after school. They were being, like I said, picked directly up from school by the scam artist.

Officer Mayo said scam operators would tell parents—mostly blue-collar workers or the poor—that they'd take the children off the parents' hands and give them paying jobs so they wouldn't be running with gangs. The parents believed it to be a good thing, but "the end result," Mayo said, "is the kids do not get an education, they flunk out of school and we got problems later on."

The fast food industry is now the largest employer of teenagers in the country. The Lantos Subcommittee decided in 1990 to hold hearings on their child labor policies. Lantos summoned the four largest fast food operators: McDonald's, Burger King, Little Caesar's, and Domino's Pizza. McDonald's in 1990 had about eighty-three hundred restaurants in the United States, employing an average of sixty people in each. About one fourth of the McDonald's are owned by the corporation; the rest are licensed to independent owners. The majority of workers are part-time hourly crew employees.

In the late 1980s, the company began hiring fourteen- and fifteen-year-olds on a limited basis. About seventeen hundred were on the payroll by 1990. That year the Wisconsin Department of Labor investigated McDonald's in Milwaukee, and cited the corporation for sixty-five violations of the state child labor law. Thirty-two children worked beyond curfew, twenty-seven worked more than eight-hour days, four worked more than forty-hour weeks, two worked without permit, and one worked during school hours. Of some two hundred restaurants inspected, about 10 percent were cited for violations.

A McDonald's spokesman told the Lantos Subcommittee the company now has a policy of commitment to education, stressing the need for flexible scheduling of young workers and sensitivity to a working student's needs. It wants to

A sixteen-year-old short-order cook at work in Salisbury, Maryland.

"ensure a balance between school and work in order to maintain or improve academic performance."

The typical young worker in a McDonald's, the spokesman said, "is not usually an upper-middle-class youngster looking to buy a second stereo, but is from a family which needs to augment its income with the earnings from part-time work."

Turning to Burger King, the second largest fast food chain in the country, Congressman Lantos said:

> Just this past week the Department of Labor charged Burger King with violating child labor laws at some of its 800 company-owned restaurants. This gives meaning to Burger King's heavily promoted "Kids Club Meals." Until this action . . . many thought the biggest risk at Burger King was eating their french toast sticks. [Laughter.]
>
> The fact that such a large employer of young people has allegedly been violating child protection laws over many years by working 14 and 15 year olds more hours than the law permits and by assigning young workers under the age of 18 to perform hazardous tasks does not speak well for past enforcement efforts by the Department of Labor.

It came out during the hearings that the Department of Labor had filed a lawsuit alleging that Burger King had repeatedly violated child labor provisions of the federal law for nearly four years in forty-two of its restaurants around the country.

Little Caesar's—the world's largest pizza carry-out chain—has some three thousand restaurants. About three fourths of them are owned and operated under franchise. In 1990, of its fifty-five thousand employees, thirteen thousand were under eighteen, most of them sixteen- and seventeen-year-olds. During the Operation Child Watch Sweep, Little Caesar's restaurants were cited for violations of the child labor law, mostly in the case of workers under the age of sixteen. The corporation's own restaurants have a policy of not hiring workers under sixteen. All the violations occurred in the franchises.

Congressman Lantos pointed out that all four corporations had the power to revoke a franchise, but had never used it against franchisees for a pattern of serious violations of child labor laws. Obviously they were reluctant to lose profits by doing that. Again and again, Lantos pressed them to do more than express regret at violations. Not talk, but *action* was needed.

"The most neglected area of child labor abuse in the U.S.," according to the National Safe Workplace Institute, is the fast food industry. "Unfortunately, the demands of work for too many youths in this industry have taken a priority over the interests of school, family and community."

If They Can Get Away with It

Back in the early 1900s, illegal child labor was found mostly in factories, where youngsters worked on machines. Today, however, there is far less of that, for American industry has moved a vast amount of its production to countries where wages and taxes are much lower—and profits, therefore, are much higher.

But high profits can still be made in the States—especially in sweatshops. Few Americans are aware that the industrial sweatshops exposed by the crusading reporters at the turn of the century (see chapter 7) have been flourishing again since the late 1970s. They are found in cities coast to coast where new immigrants have flooded in. Eager for work, often without legal papers, unable to speak English and ignorant of the law, they are the victims of ruthless employers seeking cheap and pliant labor. You find them in many businesses, most of them small, doing laundry, or making clothing, costume jewelry, toys, or electronic parts. The shops are often hidden from the law—not just from Department of Labor inspectors, but from tax collectors and union organizers as well. Says Jeffrey Newman of the National Child Labor Committee: "If the employers can get away with it, they will break the child labor laws. And they *can* get away with it."

In 1990, more than fifty thousand people were employed in New York State in forty-five hundred sweatshops in the clothing industry alone. And many of the workers were children. It's almost impossible to detect the children because many work at home, not in a factory.

A Vietnamese woman, determined to fight industrial homework, reported on sweatshop conditions to her Vietnamese community. She tells what she saw during one inspection:

> One weekday, I entered a four-room apartment in the Bronx. From the outset, I noticed that the apartment was very barren with only a few pieces of furniture. There were no rugs on the floor; however, there were materials strewn about. It was a visible sign of homework. It was a home consisting of a Vietnamese mother and four children, of whom two are Amerasians. The mother is middle-age while the children range from 12–17 with perhaps one year apart in age. While I was talking to the mother, the children—1 boy, 3 girls were working on the floor in a remarkably

ordered manner. One child was in charge of sewing the bows on an old machine in one corner of the room. The materials are then passed to another child who reverses and cuts the excess off the bow materials, which are then passed to the next who glued the bows with a gun. The final step was to place hair clips on the bows which was supervised by the young boy. It was an organized and practiced routine.

With frankness, the mother described their schedule. She attends ESL classes in the morning while the children attend the nearby junior and high schools. In the afternoon when they come home the children would start on the work that was delivered daily. Usually the work must be done by pickup time the next day. All of the children are needed to pitch in. Quite often when the work is too much the children have to stay up most of the night to finish. When that occurs, they are always very sleepy and unprepared in class. With a sad expression, she stated that though she knows they are unable to keep up with their classmates, they have no choice because she is unable to work and support the whole family. Though the money they get is poor with $1.20 for a dozen of bows sometimes maybe $1.50, they can make on an average about 3–4 dozens an hour. In one good night they may make up to $40. But that is if they work most of the night. Though it is not much but with foodstamp and Medicaid they can have some spending money. Sometimes when the children complain, she must constantly reassure them that one day they will make enough to stop working like this and move away.

Situation like above I have seen often in my investigation. Most family do homework until they can save enough to move or confident enough to get off welfare. However, this kind of mentality persists and they continue to work at home for years. In the meantime, the children suffer and usually do not go on after high school due to academic deficiency. It is a shame in these children's cases because being Americans they deserve more for their future in the land of their father.

Immigrants from everywhere are exploited in the same way. An investigator reported he went into a building on Manhattan's West Side and saw "a 15-year-old Mexican immigrant boy working in conditions considered barbarous half a century ago. He could be found by his table sewing pleats into cheap, white chiffon skirts. He hopes to make a dollar an hour."

Ships from mainland China sail into American ports carrying human cargo destined for labor in the restaurants and sweatshops of America's Chinatowns. Smuggled mostly out of southern China—at high prices—they are poor farmers and laborers following those nineteenth-century Chinese immigrants who built America's transcontinental railroad. They, too, are in search of prosperity. To pay off the cost

Young workers in a garment factory in New York's Chinatown.

of their passage, they end up in restaurants, packinghouses, and garment factories.

Those who reached New York City have turned its Chinatown into the city's clothing manufacturing center. Nearly six hundred garment factories operate in the crowded tenements of New York's oldest slum. Working a six-day week, from sixty to eighty hours, is typical, and for less than $200 a week. Most workers make the minimum wage of $4.25 an hour. When piece rates drop, they try to recover the lost wages by putting in longer hours. Many of the Chinese mothers—illegals—have their children, some as young as five, working alongside them. You see these kids working as thread trimmers or standing by the machines, handing their mothers bundles of cloth.

The worst sweatshops are basement operations with no exit doors. Children of seven and eight work fifty to sixty hours a week, at way below minimum wage. Bosses also let workers take sewing home—a big violation of the law. Whole families pitch in, seven days a week, to get the job done. Employers may pay the family in checks that bounce and then call immigration officials to raid the place. The workers are too scared to complain. If they do, they are blacklisted and then get no work in Chinatown.

The Department of Labor in 1942 declared industrial homework illegal. But beginning in the Reagan years the department began to loosen the regulations. This is done by talking the language of free enterprise, claiming it's the right of people to choose where and when they will work. But the dark side of that "freedom" is that industrial homework leads all too easily to exploiting children. Studies show that this kind of work can go on for long hours and occur under poor conditions of light, space, and ventilation. "At the very least," says Dr. Philip J. Landrigan, "such work impairs a child's development and education, and at the worst, it causes injury and illness."

At a congressional hearing, Dr. Landrigan said:

> To be sure, healthy work supervised in a safe en-
> vironment for a limited number of hours and
> under safe conditions can be good for the develop-
> ment of children. Such work is to be encouraged.
> It is a part of teaching children life's work.
>   But the labor of children for long hours under
> the kitchen lights, sewing, stitching, carrying

thread and moving cloth into the night while schoolwork remains undone and while sleep is kept at bay, is bad, unhealthy, dangerous, and barbaric. It is associated with exposure to toxins and carcinogens, such as formaldehyde. It is associated with cuts and needle injuries. School principals report to us that industrial homework is associated with previously bright and alert children falling asleep at their desks and failing to learn.

But child labor, as we noted in the last chapter, is also concentrated heavily in the service occupations and on the farm. Let's look at the work young people do in agriculture.

Start with the story of Augustino Nieves, a fourteen-year-old boy born in Mexico whose family moved to California. At thirteen, he started working alongside his parents. With the help of a translator, he told the Lantos Subcommittee what his life as a migrant farm worker was like:

> I have been working in the fields of California for the past two years. We began by picking grapes in Madeira and then moved to Orland where we pick olives. I was unable to begin school in September 1989 because we were still working in the fields. I was not able to enroll in school until January 1990. I missed three months of school.

Augustino wanted to work in the same crew with his father, but the company didn't want to hire him. They said he needed a permit to work. So he went to the company where his uncle worked and they hired him. They knew he did not have an official permit or even a social security card, but they hired him.

My job consists of moving up and down long rows of strawberry plants, bent over looking for strawberries. I pick only the good strawberries and place them in a packing box. I move my push cart up and down the field. I may spend the whole day working in a stooped position.

When there are a lot of ripe strawberries in the field our crew begins working at 6:30 A.M. and continues working till 8 P.M. We work 6 days a week. The boss does not pay us by the hour.

On a good day, I can pick about 30 boxes of strawberries. If the strawberries are for the market, they pay us $1.25 a box. If I work really hard, I can make about $36.50 for a 13-hour day. That comes out to about $2.80 an hour.

The conditions in the field are oftentimes very difficult. Since we are working on a piece-rate basis, the boss does not allow us to take 15-minute breaks in the morning or afternoon. We have to work through our breaks. We take only 20 minutes for lunch. By the end of the day, our backs hurt and we are very tired.

The boss is supposed to have clean bathrooms and water for us out in the field. However, there are many days when there are no bathrooms in the field. When there are bathrooms, they are usually

several hundred meters away from us, and oftentimes they are very dirty. The boss puts the bathrooms so far away because he wants to discourage
us from taking breaks.

The boss often didn't provide them with drinking water.
When they were lucky enough to have water, instead of
having disposable drinking cups, they all used the same cup.

One of the worst things about working in the
strawberry fields is that every eight days, the
ranchers apply sulfur to the fields as a pesticide.
When we bend over to pick the strawberries, the
sulfur gets into our eyes. The sulfur stings our
eyes and burns our throats. We have been working—we have to keep working even though we
are in great pain.

The foreman always puts great pressure on us
to work as fast as we can. The foreman comes up
behind us and yells at us to work faster and faster.
Oftentimes, he insults me because I am a Mixtec
Indian. They scream, "Hurry up, work faster, you
Pinche Oaxequeno." The foreman especially puts
a lot of pressure on me because I still cannot work
as fast as an adult man.

We face many indignities in the field. We know
that the boss exploits us. However, we cannot
complain or the foreman will fire us. There are
plenty of people who want our jobs, and we have
to put up with these abuses or we will not be able
to work.

I wish I did not have to work in the fields but my family needs all the money that I can earn. When my whole family is working in the fields, we can eat meat and drink sodas. When there is no work, we only eat tortillas and beans.

My father has many responsibilities. I have three younger siblings who are still in Mexico, and we need to send them money so they can eat and go to school. My father also has to pay a lot of money for rent. The rent of our apartment is $750 a month. About 25 people live in our three-bedroom apartment.

My parents, my sister and myself all sleep on the floor in one of the bedroms. Next fall, I will begin my first year of high school. Hopefully, my family will be able to stay in Santa Maria for the whole school year.

My dream is to graduate from high school. However, if my family ever needs me to go out to work in the fields, that is where I will be.

Here are some basic facts about child labor on the farm: The Department of Labor estimates there are 277,500 children age fifteen or over working in the fields. (No data are available on the number fourteen or under who are working.) This is the low estimate. At the high end, the United Farm Workers Union estimates there are 800,000 children working as hired farm labor in America. According to the American Friends Service Committee, one fourth of all farm labor in this country is performed by children.

Chicano children picking fruit in a California orchard.

As for earnings, a study made for the U.S. Department of Labor held that an average migrant-worker family in 1989 had an income of $5,000 to $7,500. The poorest workers were in the Southeast, primarily Florida. Few find work in that state for more than thirty weeks a year. Migrating north gives them another ten to fifteen weeks.

Who are these people? A survey made in Immokalee, Florida, home of one of the nation's largest concentrations of migrant workers, showed they included Mexicans, Mexican Americans, African Americans, Haitians, and Guatemalan Indians.

Do farm workers *want* their kids to work in the fields? William G. Hoerger, a staff lawyer for the California Rural Legal Assistance Program, discussed that with the Lantos Subcommittee. He said there are tens of thousands of unemployed farm workers in his state and that "employers have taken advantage of workers' desperation for jobs by lowering wage levels and eliminating benefits often below legal requirements."

At the same time, the growers have greatly increased their use of farm labor contractors, often unlicensed, who compete for the growers' business. They "underbid each other to the point where neither minimum wage nor other mandatory remedial benefits can be provided if the contractor is to earn any profit." Paid even less than the minimum wage, the farm workers are forced to bring their children—kids ages nine, ten, or eleven—to work with them. So it is a basic matter of survival for the farm workers' families. The children's work goes into the parents' work record. It may be at so low a piece rate that their pay drops way down to as little as $1 per hour. Farm workers are the lowest paid occupational group in America.

You may wonder why children working in agriculture are denied the same protection that the law offers to children in other workplaces. The reason goes back to the struggle in 1938 to pass the Fair Labor Standards Act. As with most legislation, compromise between conflicting interests or groups was necessary. To gain as much protection as possible for the greatest number of workers, Congress made a deal. The farm bloc promised its vote if farm workers were left out of the bill. That set a precedent that has hung on in many states for more than fifty years. The unfair double standard Congress accepted has kept down the wages and working conditions of farm workers ever since.

It is a sad thing to realize that the same child labor violations for which thousands of employers have been cited are okay on the farm. Yet who can deny that children working on a farm deserve the same protection?

You can see why from the experience of Dr. Paul M. Monahan. He practiced medicine in the Yakima Valley Farm Workers Clinic in Oregon. This is what he saw one day:

> I was called to the Emergency Room to evaluate a 14-year-old boy who had been injured while working in hop harvest. A tractor had driven over his head. He had fallen asleep in the mid-afternoon from exhaustion . . . exhaustion from having been involved in a hop harvest campaign, working 12 to 14 hour days, 80-plus hours per week. Miraculously, he was not severely injured

since his head had been in a depressed furrow in
the field. His terror was justified by the tractor
treads across his forehead. I was reminded of this
episode when a second 14-year-old boy was killed;
his head was crushed by a tractor in hop harvest.
He too had fallen asleep. After all, it was 2 in the
morning in mid-September. In the daytime he was
attending school. . . .

And then there was the Saturday afternoon
when I was called to the Emergency Room again
to try to resuscitate a 16-year-old boy who had
been electrocuted along with two other workers.
The farmer was using them to help construct a
grain bin—the heavy equipment boom hit power
lines and the three workers were instantly killed.
Had this work activity been defined as construction work rather than inappropriately labeled, "agricultural work," then the employer would have
suffered severe penalties. Since it was merely agriculture, apparently there were no violations. Had
it been construction, the 16-year-old wouldn't
have been in that situation.

And then there was the youngster (4 years old?)
who was decapitated by a passing automobile as
his family was crossing an unpaved road to begin
asparagus harvest between 4 and 5 in the morning: He is probably included as a motor vehicle/
pedestrian statistic rather than an agricultural victim. Another Clinic physician had to deal with the
grieving parents. And the tractor crush-death of

my son's high school friend—but then he was 18
or 19 years old.

Such catastrophes are fortunately uncommon. The fact is
that they are also unnecessary and should not occur.

Then there is the story of how young Keith Adams died.
Here is the voice of his mother, Marilyn Adams, a family
farmer:

> We gave our little boy an adult responsibility and
> left him unattended and he didn't know how to
> react. He didn't know what was dangerous and he
> didn't know what to do when he got himself into
> that situation and he was alone. The day that
> Keith died I had no idea that flowing grain was
> dangerous. My son was 11 and he had stayed
> home from school one day to help his dad harvest
> the corn and his dad didn't have any extra help
> that day and Keith was pretty good help and they
> were good buddies and so he'd helped him all day
> long. He was unloading a gravity flow wagon and
> climbed up on top of this wagon while it was un-
> loading and immediately was just pulled under
> like quicksand. Darrell came back in from the
> field and saw that the wagon wasn't loaded and
> there was just a trickle of grain coming out the
> door and he saw Keith's feet.

Keith had suffocated in the flowing grain.

Of every five deaths on family farms, one is a child under

the age of sixteen. A 10-year-old can drive a big tractor down a highway without a license. That's legal. Should the tractor tip over or cause injury, in most states it won't be reported as a workplace accident. It falls outside the federal child labor laws.

In Iowa, Jeris and Otto Petersen ran a 430-acre farm. One hot July day, their son Shaun pitched in to help his dad. Otto tells what happened:

> We were just going to finish cleaning out the bin and there's a power sweep-over that goes—circles the bin and Shaun was inside shoveling corn— probably just the last 10 scoops of corn. It was hot and he was sweating. I told him to come out and I would finish it. He come to the window and I told him I'd be there in a second and then I turned my back and I was going to shut the grinder off and about that time, the sweep-over come around and caught Shaun's shoe and he got wrapped up in the sweep-over.

Shaun was rushed to the hospital and 20 minutes later was pronounced dead. The grain bin he died in was abandoned. Nobody in the family could go back down there. For the Adamses and the Petersens, losing a child was a tragedy with no ending.

In 1989 *The Wall Street Journal* reported that 300 children die of farm-related accidents each year and that over 23,500 are injured. Here are additional facts about the effects of farm labor on children's health:

- Nearly 50 percent of children working in the fields have been sprayed with pesticides.

- Two studies have linked childhood brain tumors and leukemia to pesticide exposure.

- The infant mortality rate is 125 percent higher for migrant workers than the national average.

- The rate of parasitic infection among migrant workers is estimated to be eleven to fifty-nine times higher than that of the general U.S. population.

- The incidence of malnutrition among migrant workers is higher than among any other subpopulation in this country.

I Looked Up, and My Leg Wasn't There

We've seen the risks run by children working on the farm. Child labor in the cities, suburbs, and small towns can be just as perilous. At fifteen, Jennifer Forshee worked in a Burger King in Santa Rosa, California. She tells what happened to her:

> I cut the tip of my right finger off. The reason for this was because the machine I was using was broken, and I was forced to use my hand instead of the tool that pushed the vegetables down into the food processor. The only training I ever received on this machine was how to turn the machine itself on and how to make the salads look pretty. . . . I feel that this Burger King was very irresponsible. . . . I was only 15 at the time and I

do not feel that I should have been the one to say
that I should not have been on this machine.

Jennifer said that no one—neither her employer nor her
school—told her anything about the child labor laws and
what her rights were under those laws. She worked twenty-
five to thirty hours a week during the school year, and
sometimes fifty a week in summertime. She didn't work
because her family needed help, but to earn money for a
car.

Jesse Colson was a seventeen-year-old Indiana boy who
died in 1989 while making a delivery for Domino's Pizza.
His mother, Mrs. Suzanne Boutros, told a congressional
committee what happened to her son:

> Domino's has a policy of guaranteeing the deliv-
> ery of a pizza within 30 minutes from the time an
> order is placed. To deliver their product, Domi-
> no's relies on young people whom they hire as
> drivers. I wish that someone at Domino's corpo-
> rate headquarters had taken 30 minutes to think
> about the sensibility of their policy. That 30 min-
> utes just may have saved my son's life.
>
> Jesse had been job-hunting without success
> when he learned that the Mooresville Domino's
> store was hiring. When he went to the store to
> apply, he was told by the manager that if he had a
> driver's license and a car, the job was his. Jesse
> had been working for Domino's for approxi-
> mately 3 weeks when he slid off the road one
> night in January—this was an icy curve—he was

making his last delivery of the night on his way home. . . .

By the end of April, I noticed that Jesse's driving habits were not as good as they had been. He would leave for work in plenty of time to get there but he seemed to be in a big hurry anyway. When my husband and I questioned him about this, he began to talk about the pressure he was feeling. I could see that he was pressured just by looking at him.

We also began to question the distance he was having to go to deliver these pizzas. Some friends of ours live a good 7 miles from the store where he worked, and 7 miles is a long way when a young person is under a time restriction. Jesse was not getting enough sleep during this time due to the late hours he was working. He would be so "wired" when he came home at night that it took him a while to relax just so he could fall asleep. It was becoming apparent to me that the whole Domino's work ethic was a recipe for disaster.

Finally, his mother told Jesse he needed to find another job—that this one just wasn't worth it. Not only was he under too much pressure and not getting enough sleep, he was also tearing up his car and wasn't receiving enough gas money from his employment for the deliveries each night. He agreed and he did find another job, which he would have started the following Monday, June 5.

On Saturday, June 3, the day of Jesse's death, I had let him sleep in because he had worked late the night before. When he got up he told me he had been having clutch trouble the night before and he went to check it out. He discovered that his car had a flat and by the time he got it repaired that day he was running late for work. As he ran out the door, he asked me to call his manager to let him know that he was running late. That was the last time I saw him alive.

During the day, it had begun to storm and by that evening there was water standing in the streets and roads. Mooresville is a rural area with badly paved roads, they're rough, they're curvy, they're winding. The site of the accident was exactly 3 miles from the Mooresville store, and I don't know where he was headed that night, but it was apparent that it was some distance further than the accident site.

From what the police officers could tell, Jesse was driving too fast and he came upon a small rise in the road with standing water. He hydroplaned and became airborne. The officer told me there was no way he could have controlled the vehicle, which was a Toyota pickup truck that belonged to the store.

The truck wrapped around an enormous utility pole and Jesse, who wasn't wearing his seatbelt, was thrown between the door and the doorframe and killed instantly. His aorta was ruptured.

Officers told me that it wasn't likely that a seat-belt would have saved his life.

Dozens of such needless accidents could be added. In Laurel, Maryland, Matthew Garvey, thirteen, went to work in a car wash. He was sucked into the towel-drying machine. It spun him around and spit him out. He remembers "lying on the street and looking up, and my leg wasn't there, it was in the dryer."

In East Stroudsburg, Pennsylvania, Michael Hucorne, seventeen, was working part-time in the Weis Food Market. One afternoon he began operating a compactor baling machine. He tried to reach into the machine to take out paper materials that had been caught during the baling process. But there was no way to stop the upward movement of the ram once it began its cycle and Michael became wedged in near the top of the machine. There were no instructions, at, on, or near the machine on how to stop it during its cycle or in case of emergency. Finally, after frantic calls to the manufacturer of the machine, people trying to save Michael cut the hydraulic hoses and took his body from the machine. But it was too late. He died of compression asphyxiation after being in the machine more than thirty minutes.

A fifteen-year-old boy named Kevin Curley died in a bakery accident in West Pittston, Pennsylvania. He was accidentally killed shortly after midnight while cleaning a horizontal dough-mixing machine, although he was hired supposedly only to bag rolls. He had been employed in violation of the state's child labor laws. He didn't have

An underage meatpacker unjamming machinery in a New York City supermarket.

working papers, he stayed on the job after permitted hours, and he was paid in cash "under the table" for a flat amount each evening.

Even working in a grocery store poses risks. It's legal work for those age fourteen and up, and such stores in the cities rely heavily on a young work force. Where space for stock is scarce, managers stack items to a great height and kids fall off ladders or are hurt by falling objects. Cuts are caused by cardboard boxes and the knives used to open them. Although the law bars children from operating the machines used to crush or bale those boxes, an eleven-year-old boy in the Bronx was killed when he was entangled in a box crusher.

In the fast food trade, minor lacerations and burns are quite common dangers. One boy died of electrocution because of a power outlet on a wet floor in an improperly grounded building. The heavy use of microwave equipment in fast food places tends to damage the seals of food ovens, which can cause excessive microwave exposure. Such exposure to high doses may cause eye damage that leads to the formation of cataracts.

Well, how often do these accidents occur? Are the examples given here exceptional? Studies made by the General Accounting Office (GAO) revealed that during 1987–1988, thirty-three states (the other seventeen were not included in the report) reported that forty-eight child workers were killed and 128,000 were injured in the workplace. And that's only part of the story. Senator Howard M. Metzenbaum, chair of a Senate subcommittee dealing with child labor, says that "the GAO studies underestimate the true magni-

tude of workplace injuries to children because no com-
prehensive work-related injury and illness data exist for
minors."

It has been demonstrated that there is a strong link between the injury rate of working children and child labor
violations. In 1990, the state of Washington ran a survey of
work-related child injuries. It concluded that 44 percent of
all injuries to children occurred while those children were
working in violation of the Fair Labor Standards Act. If you
take only those young people most seriously hurt, you find
that 57 percent of them were working in violation of the
protections of the law.

The facts are damning. Don't employers care what happens to children?

Work—or Education?

Working, everyone agrees, can be a valuable part of growing up. But how often is that the case? Is every job a genuine apprenticeship for adulthood?

Those who study the question find that child labor often interferes seriously with school performance.

Even those students who muster enough energy not to fall asleep find their work schedule denies them the chance to take part in after-school activities and sports. Child labor interferes with play, too. And play is important to every stage of growing up. Time to relax and just have fun is necessary for children to grow and learn.

What do young people learn from employers? For some it may be something quite harmful. When children are hired without working papers and asked to "work off the books," required to work after midnight, or told to work on legally banned machinery, they get the impression it's okay to break the law. And as we've already noted, they see many employers getting away with it.

Ever since the mid-1960s, more and more high-school students have been taking jobs. At any given time, more than half of them work and another fourth are looking for work. By the time they are high-school seniors, 80 to 90 percent of students will have worked while attending school. We've seen that most of the jobs they get are low-skilled and offer little training. In exchange for short-term wage gains, student workers—and society—are giving up investment in the future by not learning critical skills at school.

In some places, however, there is an effort to provide formal programs of combined work and study, and cooperative education programs as well. A prime example is Junior Achievement. It's a nonprofit organization started

A child being helped with schoolwork by a Junior Achievement staffer.

more than seventy years ago, dedicated to teaching young people about the world of business. Its emphasis in recent years is on preventing young people from dropping out. Its programs reach 1.2 million students in fourteen thousand schools. It recruits volunteer adult executives and sends them into the social studies or economics classroom to work with the teacher. It reaches out also to the poorest urban schools, whose students are most at risk in dropping out. In some of its programs, children even on the elementary level create and run small businesses in which they learn about planning, budgets, buying, selling, saving, and investing. Junior Achievement also has after-school projects.

The programs cost the schools nothing: corporations, foundations, gifts, and fund-raising events supply the budget. While Junior Achievement makes no claim for bringing down dropout rates, it does provide role models, activities with real results, and lessons in how the world of work and business operates. Students find out the value of staying in school. They begin to see the possibility of careers and a kind of life they may never have thought of before.

There aren't many such programs, however. Not much has yet been done to link students' actual experience on the job to their schooling.

And that's of vital importance today. For as industry and business change—and rapidly!—they demand more from their workers, especially those without college degrees. Says Paul F. Cole, a leader of the New York State AFL-CIO:

> Workers on the floor are being empowered, work-
> ing more with technology, working in self-

directed teams, doing more problem-solving and using more higher-order thinking and reasoning skills. The intellectual and skill demands of the workplace of tomorrow require major improvements in the education of the non-college-bound and the fifty percent of those who are four-year college dropouts. Our schools offer little or no assistance to those who will be directly entering the workforce. The result is that the typical high school graduate will move from one dead-end job to another.

When Cole speaks of the non-college-bound, he means the group that makes up more than half of the nation's high-school graduates and a majority of its disadvantaged and minority students. This is a group in desperate need of help in making the transition from high school to the world of work.

The choice for students is to develop high skills—or to expect only low wages. America needs to rethink the school-to-work process. What part should work have in education? A Cornell University professor, Stephen F. Hamilton, has proposed a new approach to the old apprenticeship system. He suggests linking the school and the workplace by teaching some of the same knowledge and skills in both settings.

Hamilton proposes a number of ways this could be done. One is exploratory apprenticeships in which students would engage in community service work. Another option is work in school-run enterprises, such as cafeterias or day-care centers. A third is work-based apprenticeships that would combine schooling with apprenticeship over a period spanning two years of high school and two years of technical college.

In Europe, such four-year work-study programs are common and often compulsory. They train young people for skilled jobs, turning millions of them into sophisticated entry-level workers. But there are only a handful of such programs in the United States. One reason is that, during a recession, companies find it hard to justify hiring young apprentices when they are laying off skilled workers. More important, companies that do spend much on worker training invest in existing employees, not in a future work force of apprentices still in high school. Also, American companies are competing in world markets by simplifying work and lowering wage costs. They are reluctant to take on school apprentices.

By contrast, about three hundred thousand young people already out of high school are in apprenticeship programs to become licensed carpenters, electricians, bricklayers, and the like. So far, it's mostly hospitals very short of technicians, and manufacturers equally short of skilled machinists or metalworkers, who have embraced school apprenticeship projects.

Although education-for-work projects are a good idea, some cautions are necessary. Many employers need only a low-skilled work force. A national study made in 1990 found an estimated 5 percent of employers organizing work so as to require a high level of skilled workers. Investigators of youth apprenticeship programs report that students in some of them learn few academic or technical skills. And employers who want an obedient work force don't encourage students to think critically about the workplace. To get businesses interested in cooperating, schools may let them veto anything threatening in the classroom. School administrators and teachers in turn may censor themselves in order to win business support.

An ideal youth apprenticeship program would let students rotate through a variety of work experiences while in high school, rather than have them become fixed to a single occupational area. They ought to be exposed to nonprofit community services and small businesses, as well as to large corporations.

There are programs that develop both work skills and citizenship skills at the same time. One example is Middle College High School at LaGuardia Community College in New York City. Students in its ninth, tenth, and twelfth grades spend thirteen weeks a year at a job. While doing this, they return to class one day a week to talk about labor and union issues, business links to the community, and worker skills and attitudes. Their learning is broadened and enriched as they compare what they've experienced in a variety of workplaces.

Another proposal for improving the education-to-work experience comes from Thomas Y. Hobart, Jr., a leader of a teachers' organization in New York State. He suggests:

1. The issuance of work permits should be tied to academic standards similar to the criteria developed in many school districts for participation in sports.
2. At the time of initial employment, employers should contact the school to determine the students' grades and potential academic problems. The employers could follow

up with school personnel throughout the school year to determine if the work experience is hindering the students' academic success and to develop ways that the experience could be connected to the students' schooling.

3. Local business concerns should work with school administrators and teachers in how best to provide sound work experience that is not harmful to students' school performance but relates to and enhances their knowledge and skills.

4. Employers should play a part in motivating students to give more time to studies and to limit their work hours.

In other words, the basic occupation for all young people should be their education. But for schools and the workplaces to be matched will take much greater cooperation between schools and local employers than you find now. Schools don't know much about the workplace, especially as it changes. And employers know little about education and schools.

A lot more needs to be done to improve schooling and training for minority children coming into the work force. After the Los Angeles riots of 1992, public officials woke to the fact that minority workers will represent more than half the growth in the labor force in the next decade. But how well equipped are those workers for the demanding jobs of the twenty-first century? Economists say that America will pay the price in lower growth in productivity if something isn't done soon to tackle the problem of poor education and training. If things go on as they have, it will mean a lower standard of living—not just for minorities— but for all Americans.

Minority youths—many of them dropouts or graduates of inferior schools—need special efforts and funding to prepare them for work. Many grow up in an atmosphere of poverty, violence, and despair. The level of poverty among American children is more than twice that of any other industrial country. And most American youths—whites as well as nonwhites—are less prepared for the workplace than youths in other industrial nations. At the same time, the United States does less to help youths make the transition from school to the workplace.

Economists and educators think the time is more than ripe for Congress to take action that would help young people make that transition from school to the workplace. One proposal calls for setting up a tough national academic standard for all students that they could be expected to meet by the age of sixteen. For dropouts, job-training programs would be financed that would also provide remedial education in the basics.

Looking at what has worked so well in Germany, it is suggested that government establish a broad range of technical and professional certificates. These would go to young people who don't enter college, but instead complete programs of work and study linked to occupations. The certificates would demonstrate that their holders have entry-level skills for specific occupations.

A carryover from the War on Poverty of the 1960s is the Job Corps. Started under President Lyndon B. Johnson in 1964, its aim is to transform some of the most disadvantaged sixteen- to twenty-two-year-olds into skilled, responsible workers. It's a unique partnership between public and private agencies. The U.S. Department of Labor sets the program guidelines. Foundations, universities, unions, Y's, federal agencies such as the Department of the Interior or Department of Agriculture, and corporations run the centers, and unions and trade groups train the students and help them find work. The government provides the facilities and equipment.

The training is offered in a variety of fields, including automotive trades, carpentry, bricklaying, electrical trades, welding, nursing, clerical and secretarial skills, and food service skills—in fact, more than 160 different jobs. The Job Corps centers are a mix of vocational training, boarding school, and boot camp. They have been widely praised for being effective and cost-efficient. But in the early 1990s, they were training only sixty-two thousand young men and women a year—less than 6 percent of the eligible popula-

Young people in a Job Corps center mastering food-service skills.

tion. This is evidence of how the corps has had to fight for funding, or even for bare existence, again and again.

There have been proposals calling for fifty additional centers by the year 2000. The Urban League calls for vastly expanding the Job Corps to four hundred thousand young people a year.

Entrants to the Job Corps are drawn by recruiting posters, broadcast advertising, and social workers. The schooling in the centers allows students to progress at their own pace in reading and math, while they learn basic social and workplace skills, including how to handle criticism and how to act at job interviews. While at the center, students can earn a high school equivalency diploma (GED). On average, students stay in a center for about ten months.

The results so far? Following up, the Job Corps finds 67 percent of the graduates get jobs and 17 percent go on to higher education.

"Job Corps is the only thing that seems to make a difference," according to Gordon Berlin of the Manpower Demonstration Research Corporation. "This is right under our noses, and it's surprising to me we haven't given it more time or attention. It's a very valuable resource we could draw on. Why not double Job Corps?"

All Around the World

What about child labor outside the United States?

Look just south of us, across the border into Mexico, and you'll see boys and girls exploited as badly as, or worse than, here at home. On the outskirts of Juárez, a city across the river from El Paso, Texas, the dry brown hills are lined with mile after mile of crude huts. They are just big boxes made of cardboard and packing cases, with tarpaper roofs and an outhouse in the back. Few have running water or electricity, the streets are unpaved, and there is no sewage system.

Yet the people who live in such squalid villages work for some of America's leading corporations: Ford, General Motors, Honeywell, General Electric, RCA. These are among the 1,300 industrial plants growing up along the border since the 1970s. In Juárez alone, there are some 250 plants, employing a hundred thousand Mexicans. And most of them are young: thirteen, fourteen, fifteen, sixteen—the majority of them girls.

They live in the slums of Juárez because they can't afford anything better. Their wages are as low as 55 cents an hour. And the promise that their incomes would rise in time has been cruelly hollow. Instead, incomes have been falling for years. The people can't buy the great variety of things they make and can barely afford the basic necessities of life. Because of low wages, the intensive speedup of production, and the intolerable living conditions, there's constant burnout. Many of the boys and girls quit jobs within a few months. They rove around Mexico from one bad job to another, hoping for something better.

How did this happen? It's an effect of the rapidly expanding global economy. When American companies move jobs to Mexico (or to many other places in the world), they escape higher wages, and also U.S. laws and taxes. They don't have to abide by U.S. standards of health and safety on the job. They have no commitments to the communities where they set up their factories.

Back home, wages of American workers fall, too. The people who work at the premium industrial jobs in the United States are fired when the plant is closed and production moves abroad. Or they are obliged to settle for lower wages as their unions give in to heavy pressure. If they are lucky enough to find another job, it is almost always for much lower pay.

How different is it for young workers in other countries?

Take Indonesia. Workers as young as twelve and thirteen are found in glass, textile, mosquito coil, and other industries. In one factory, a visitor saw over half the work force were children earning 70 cents a day. Supervisors hid them in toilets and large container boxes when government inspectors showed up.

A recent report from the International Labor Office (ILO)—an organization associated with the United Nations—says that in China alone there are forty million child workers age ten to fourteen.

In the underdeveloped countries, children may work sixteen hours a day, seven days a week, under miserable conditions, and for pennies. The future for child labor in those regions looks even worse. As they develop their economies, they are pressured to lower their labor costs even more in order to meet competition on the world market.

Boys bought or stolen from their parents work virtually as slaves on the carpet looms of India. Children as young as eight work twelve, fourteen, sixteen hours a day, every day of the week, every week of the year. They sit on rough planks knotting colored yarns around the stretched cords of the loom's warp. They create carpets Indian manufacturers sell around the world at a good profit. The United States is their biggest customer. Estimates of the children's work force in this industry range from three hundred thousand to over a million.

A *New York Times* reporter found the children making carpets are often beaten with sticks if they don't learn fast enough. They are kept locked up in adobe dormitories, sleep on mats on the dirt floor, are given no vegetables or milk,

Children at work on a silkworm farm in India.

and are not even allowed to take a bath. Only rarely do the boys escape their servitude. They are too young, too far from home, too scared.

Children labor in India's quarries, too, in brass smelting, in glass factories, and in match and explosive plants under dangerous, unhealthy, and oppressive conditions— and often for less than $1 a day. This, despite a law banning children under the age of fourteen from a broad range of industries. But no one has ever been jailed for breaking this law. In most cases, children are bought from their impoverished parents ($50 a child) or merely taken with the promise of future payments.

The ILO reported that in 1992 India had forty-four million child laborers nationwide.

Yes, children are badly exploited almost everywhere,

especially in three economic sectors: agriculture, small enterprise, and domestic service. As in the past, most of the world's working children are employed in agriculture. Industrialized farming is taking hold everywhere. Just as in America, it is changing production methods and the way rural families earn their living. Country folk no longer have land of their own, or now have too little of it to support themselves. They have to work for others. And the children work as long and as hard as their parents to ensure family survival. Work has kept them unschooled and illiterate. With the increased use of dangerous farm machinery and chemicals, the incidence of injury and illness among children has risen. Many exploited children flee to the already overburdened cities, where they add to a young and vulnerable work force.

Small businesses in the urban areas grow as they are fed by migration from the countryside. Most are exempted from or not covered by regulations governing larger enterprises. Children are found in such work as brickmaking, construction, handicrafts, and food services. The risks to children are great in some occupations. In brickyards, kids carry heavy loads that weaken, injure, or deform them. In carpet-weaving shops, they ruin their eyesight and damage their limbs and backs. In pencil making they breathe harmful slate dust, leading to death from lung disease.

Some child workers are independent operators. Many are in street trades—selling vegetables from a road stand, shining shoes outside hotels, washing cars, even prostitution. Little is done to protect these children from violence and abuse.

A boy loading a fifth heavy brick onto a young girl's back in a brick factory in Bogota, Colombia.

The most exploited children of all are youngsters working as domestic servants. There are thought to be huge numbers of them, particularly in Africa, Asia, and Latin America, although it's impossible to count them. The vast majority are girls, often preteens. They live with and are totally dependent on their employers. Their number is growing because of increasing poverty in these regions and the refusal of adult women to work under such bad conditions.

Some of these girls are placed by poor parents with people who say they'll support and educate the children in return for their labor—a promise often ignored. Others are hired out for wages paid usually to the parents. And some desperate parents even sell their children into bondage for cash. In such cases, parent and child may never meet again.

At their employers' mercy, child domestics typically work long hours and often without any day off. Many are given so little food, they become malnourished. They are provided with neither room nor bed and sleep on the kitchen floor. Both sexual and physical abuse are said to be common.

One international study holds that some two hundred million children under age fifteen are employed worldwide, and that many have no legal means to protect themselves from exploitation in the workplace. Besides the great damage to the children themselves, harm is done to adult workers in the United States and other developed countries where jobs are endangered by imports produced cheaply by child labor abroad.

In Congress some proposals have been made to remove "duty-free treatment" from countries which don't afford their citizens internationally recognized worker rights—in this case, a minimum age for the employment of children. By not invoking trade penalties, the United States becomes a "silent partner" in global child abuse.

Attempts to regulate child labor internationally go back as far as 1919. The ILO has often dealt with this issue. In 1973, a code it adopted summarized a dozen earlier agreements on child labor. As of 1992, more than thirty nations in many parts of the world had ratified it.

But not the United States.

Can Something Be Done?

If we lived in an ideal world, we wouldn't worry about the harm that can be done to children who work. Just think: if all young people grew up in economically secure families; if their families were loving and supportive; if they went to schools that challenged their minds, encouraged their growth, developed their talents and skills; if after completing their studies they were assured of entry-level jobs and opportunities for advancement, without regard to age, sex, national origin, or color . . . if all these were true, it would be the best of all possible worlds.

But that is not the world we live in.

The real America is a nation where:

- The richest 1 percent of families control more wealth than the bottom 90 percent.

- The wealth of the top one fifth of households *rose* by 14 percent since 1980, while the bottom four fifths *fell* by 23 percent, according to the 1990 census report.
- It is mostly the comfortable, well-off people who vote and have political influence.
- More and more Americans feel they are outside the system.
- The climb out of poverty has become harder in the last twenty years.
- The economy has been less welcoming to the young, the unskilled, and the less educated.
- Racism has become America's most persistent disease.
- The income gap between black and white Americans continues to increase.
- Young families with children have significantly less money than such families did a generation ago, a trend especially true for young black and Hispanic families and for those families with little education.
- Increasing numbers of the poor—one in four—are children.
- Nearly six million children under the age of twelve—or one out of every eight—go hungry each year.
- One in four homeless people in cities is a child.
- Half of America's seventeen-year-olds do not have reading, math, and science skills that would allow them to perform tasks required in many kinds of jobs.

- In sum, people fear that something has gone terribly wrong and that their future and their children's future are in real trouble.

What's unequal, what's unfair, are hard facts of life. It's important to know these things—but to do more than remember them. We must think about what could be done to remedy the inequities of life in our society. No political or economic program would remove all inequities—not in a year, not in the four years of any president's term in office. Because programs don't work miracles. The problems we are aware of are too deep-rooted for that. Yet what *can* be done would make a significant difference in the lives of young people and their families.

Government should be much more active in dealing with social problems and in stimulating economic growth. Public works programs such as the Works Progress Administration in the Great Depression of the 1930s could help to reverse the physical decay of the cities. They could provide jobs not only for millions of the unemployed adults but for inner-city youngsters between sixteen and twenty-two. This could be done through a version of the Civilian Conservation Corps of the thirties, in which young people would be first trained and then employed in the reconstruction of the cities they live in. Such a program would require a vast partnership between the federal and local governments, and unions and private businesses, to provide investment and job opportunities and training on a large scale.

Another great need is to improve the quality and scope of public education at every level. It would enable the future work force to produce more effectively, raise living standards, and meet the test of worldwide competition.

If all children, no matter what school district they live in, were guaranteed the same expenditure on their education, it would make an enormous difference. The great gap between the funding of schools in the affluent suburbs and in the inner cities and rural areas would be overcome.

Large-scale programs call for a return to stronger government regulation of business, reduced military spending, and a really progressive income tax. The basic question isn't really what can be done to create a healthy and more equitable social system, but what are people willing to pay for it?

While our nation's primary law on child labor is more than fifty years old, violations of that law are still a serious problem. Growing numbers of working children are damaged in many ways when employers ignore its provisions, evade them, or get away with insignificant penalties for violations.

Many bills have been introduced in Congress in recent years, intended to modify a single provision of the Fair Labor Standards Act of 1938 or to strengthen it comprehensively. The most extensive reform proposal was made in the House in 1991 by Congressmen Charles E. Schumer and Tom Lantos. No action was taken on their bill, HR 2076, before the 102nd Congress ended. But this summary of its provisions indicates what needs to be done to help improve the conditions of young people who work:

1. It mandates that the secretary of labor, the secretary of health and human services, and the U.S. Census Bureau cooperate in developing a statistical record of child workers, the industries in which they are employed, and injury and illness data with respect to such workers, and publish an annual report on the status of child labor in the United States.

2. It defines *minor* as one "who is under the age of 18 and who has not received a high school diploma or its equivalent" and it then provides: "No employer shall employ a minor unless the minor possesses a valid certificate of employment issued in accordance with this subsection." Issuance of such permits, which would reflect parental consent for the minor to be employed and verification of at least a minimum school attendance record, among other things, would be assigned to a state agency.

3. Hours of employment for minors would be carefully regulated, the hour restrictions for each subcategory of minors set forth in the legislation. The states would be required to report employment, accident, and illness data annually to the secretary of labor.

4. It mandates certain specific changes in the terms of the "hazardous work orders" currently established at the discretion of the secretary of labor.

5. It prohibits the employment of persons under sixteen years of age in door-to-door sales for profit.

6. It restructures the system of civil and criminal penalties and procedures for violations of child labor law.

7. It requires the secretary of labor to coordinate more closely with other federal and state agencies "having responsibility for enforcing labor, safety and health, and immigration laws."

8. It provides that the secretary of labor "shall establish an Advisory Committee for Child Labor to provide overall policy advice" with respect to labor and its application to the employment of minors.

9. It requires that the secretary of labor "punish and disseminate the names and addresses of each person who has willfully violated" the child labor provisions of the FLSA or any related regulation, explaining the nature of the violation. Such information concerning each violator will be made available "to affected school districts."

10. It would make applicable to any employer, without regard for a dollar volume test of sales, the child labor and related penalty provisions of the FLSA.

11. The bill expands the definition of "oppressive child labor" to include any employee under the age of fourteen who is employed by an employer as a migrant agricultural worker or a seasonal agricultural worker.

This bill was not acted upon by the Congress. It has been introduced again in the 103d Congress as HR1106. Will it

A young boy in Brazil carrying clay bricks from their drying place in the sun to the furnace where they will be baked.

A nine-year-old Haitian immigrant toting a heavy load on a Maryland farm.

be made law this time? Crusades to help children are not new. They often founder because children can't vote. And the parents of needy children are hardly able to make large contributions to political campaigns.

The record bears this out. There were seven White House conferences on children between 1909 and 1970. Seven presidents convened them, one for each decade. Each produced detailed reports and major recommendations that made front-page news. But the reports only gathered dust in the archives. Nothing happened in the legislative chambers.

The 1970 conference, the last one, was followed by many study commissions on children, sponsored by foundations. Their reports, too, failed to influence public policy or even shape public opinion in any lasting way.

The troubles America knows today are not the product of unseen natural forces. They are the outcome of political choices. These decisions are made in Washington by people elected to office. But who elects them? In the 1992 presidential election campaign, only 17 percent of the eligible voters in the states holding primaries came out to vote.

What about the central concern of this book, the problem of child labor? It seems to me that it is fundamentally linked to the question of what kind of society we want.

There is a clear choice.

We can continue to move in the direction we are headed: toward an economy in which the rich get richer and the poor get poorer. Or we can head in a different direction: toward revitalizing our economy with programs that would make child labor not only unprofitable but obsolete.

More than hope is needed to bring about such great

change. It has often been said that power concedes nothing without struggle. Those who deeply care about children and child labor—and there are many organizations and groups that do—must continue to work together to keep alive the struggle for decency and social justice.

What You Need to Know About Teenage Jobs

Remember: A part-time job is just that, because your most important job is your education. An education will help prepare you for better and higher-paying work as an adult.

If you are a teenager and want to work, then you, your parents, and your teachers should know what the laws are governing young workers, and what your rights are. Child labor laws regulate the types of jobs young people can have and the hours that can be worked.

Here are some questions and answers designed to help the working teenager. They refer only to the federal laws because each state's laws are different.

Q: HOW OLD MUST I BE BEFORE I WORK?

A: In most cases, you need to be at least fourteen to have a job. There are some exceptions to this minimum age requirement for such jobs as newspaper delivery and farm work.

Q: HOW MANY HOURS SHOULD I WORK?

A: The Child Labor Provisions section of the Fair Labor Standards Act sets the following rules for minors:

- There are no specific federal hourly limitations for children thirteen and younger, since the occupations permitted are restricted to domestic service, newspaper delivery, and nonhazardous work for their parents. Specific hours for these jobs are regulated by the states.

- When school is in session, fourteen- and fifteen-year-olds may work, but not during school hours and no more than three hours a day, eighteen hours a week. When school is not in session, work may not exceed eight hours a day, forty hours a week. These teens are prohibited from working before seven A.M. and after seven P.M., except during summers, when they can work until nine P.M. The types of work are also restricted.

- There are no hourly restrictions for sixteen- and seventeen-year-olds. However, there are numerous jobs involving hazardous equipment that are prohibited to them.

- There are no child labor restrictions (wage or hour) for young people working on farms owned or operated by their parents.

REMEMBER: If you work too much, your health, your grades, and your social life may well suffer.

Q: HOW LATE SHOULD I WORK?

A: Teenagers should never work past ten P.M. on a night before school. Unfortunately, many laws are unclear about this. Problems do arise when teenagers work too late into the night. In most states, there are hour limitations that require students not to work past a designated time. These laws are meant to protect the student worker.

Q: WILL MY JOB BE DANGEROUS?

A: Nowadays far more teenagers are likely to work in a fast food outlet than at any other job. A 1991 government study shows that young people working in the fast food industry have a much higher likelihood of being hurt than workers in many other industries.

Here are some of the common workplaces where teens get hurt, as well as the applicable Child Labor provisions of the Fair Labor Standards Act:

Restaurants: Fourteen- and fifteen-year-olds may not cook, bake, or be involved in any occupations that involve setting up, operating, adjusting, cleaning, oiling, or repairing power-driven food slicers and grinders, food choppers and cutters, and bakery-type mixers.

Grocery Stores: Youths under eighteen may not operate, assist in operating, set up, repair, oil, or clean any power-driven paper-product machines.

Pizza Deliveries: Youths under eighteen may not be hired for the sole purpose of making deliveries by car.

Car Wash: Children thirteen years and younger may not, under federal law, work in car washes.

Agriculture/Commercial Farm: Children under the age of twelve are prohibited from working on any farm unless it is owned by their own family.

Driving: No minor may work as a motor vehicle driver on any public road or highway; in or about any mine, including open pit mines or quarries; or at places where logging or sawmill operations are in progress. There is an exception for occasional driving of a car or light truck, as long as such driving is restricted to daylight hours and is only "occasional and incidental."

Bakeries: No minor may operate, assist in operating, set up, adjust, repair, oil, or clean any dough mixer; batter mixer; bread dividing, rounding, or molding machine; or certain power-driven bakery machines, or set up or adjust cookie or cracker machines.

Roofing: No minor shall work in roofing, including work in applying weatherproofing materials such as tar, tile, slate, metal, and shingles to roofs of buildings or other structures. No minor may work in related metalwork, such as flashing, or work on alterations, additions, maintenance, or repair of existing roofs.

REMEMBER: This list does not cover everything you might possibly run into. If in doubt about whether to operate a machine or how to operate it and keep yourself safe, ask your supervisor. Refuse to operate anything that you do not understand or that you consider potentially dangerous.

Q: WHAT SHOULD I DO IF I AM INJURED?

A: First, you should get immediate medical attention. Second, the costs associated with any job-related injury are your employer's responsibility. Your employer should have workers' compensation insurance to pay for any medical costs. If you lose pay because of your injury, then you may be entitled to a workers' compensation payment. Be sure to notify your boss and your parents of any work-related injuries.

Q: WILL A JOB HURT MY GRADES?

A: Work can be a positive experience. It can teach useful skills, discipline, money management, and human values. But earlier chapters have given ample evidence that teenagers who work too long or too late at night see their grades decline. Sometimes, in order to work, many teenagers take less difficult subjects rather than the math or sciences that can help them get better jobs as adults.

REMEMBER: While a German or Japanese teenager is home studying calculus and chemistry, a U.S. teenager is often working.

Q: WHERE CAN I GET MORE INFORMATION?

A: See the bibliography following.

Bibliography

The desire to write this book was ignited by a TV documentary seen early in 1991. Called *Danger: Kids at Work,* its portrait of child labor in America today startled me. I hadn't realized how many young boys and girls are the victims of exploitation by employers who violate the child labor laws, and by government that does all too little to enforce the laws and safeguard the health and safety of the children.

I wrote the producer, Lifetime Television, to say that I was interested in researching a book on the subject. The producer generously sent me a video of the program together with a transcript. Viewing the video again and again, I was angered by what I learned. I determined to do whatever I could to help make young people themselves aware of the risks taken on many kinds of jobs—and at the same time to arouse the public to the necessity of pressuring our legislators to protect our children.

I am grateful, first of all, to Lifetime Television. And next, to the Mount Sinai Medical Center in New York and its Department of Community Medicine for organizing the "Conference on Child Labor: Hazards and Remedies," held on May 29, 1992. I was permitted by Dr. Philip J. Landrigan, the conference director, to attend the all-day sessions and was granted interviews with many of the experts who gave papers or took part in panel discussions.

I am especially beholden to some of the participants who sent me additional information after the conference. They include Joseph A. Kinney, executive director, the National Safe Workplace Institute; Jay Mazur, president of the International Ladies Garment Workers Union; and Joy R. Simonson, staff member of the Subcommittee on Employment and Housing, the U.S. House of Representatives. I owe thanks also to the many organizations concerned with child welfare that responded to my queries with their literature and reports.

Among the members of Congress who proved very helpful in supplying the texts of hearing records were representatives Tom Lantos, Patricia Schroeder, the late Ted Weiss, and Senator Howard Metzenbaum.

Adams, Myron E. "Children in American Street Trades." *Annals of the American Academy,* May 1905.

Bailyn, Bernard. *Voyages to the West: A Passage in the Peopling of America on the Eve of Revolution.* New York: Knopf, 1987.

Bartlett, John, and James B. Steele. *America: What Went Wrong?* Kansas City, Missouri: Andrews & McMeel, 1992.

Battiscombe, Georgina. *Shaftsbury: The Great Reformer, 1801–1885.* Boston: Houghton Mifflin, 1975.

Bingham, S. "The Child Labor Sting." *Newsweek,* March 26, 1990.

Blewett, Mary H. *The Lost Generation: Work and Life in the Textile Mills of Lowell, Massachusetts, 1910–1960.* Amherst, Massachusetts: University of Massachusetts Press, 1990.

Bodnar, John. *Workers' World: Kinship, Community and Protest in an Industrial Society, 1900–1940.* Baltimore: Johns Hopkins University Press, 1992.

Bremner, Robert H., ed. *Children and Youth in America: A Documentary History, 1600–1865.* Cambridge, Massachusetts: Harvard University Press, 1970.

Bremner, Robert H. *From the Depths: The Discovery of Poverty in the United States.* New York: New York University Press, 1956.

Bridenbaugh, Carl, and Robert Bridenbaugh. *Vexed and Troubled Englishmen, 1590–1642.* New York: Oxford University Press, 1968.

Brock, W. C. "How to Stop Child Labor Law Abuses." *USA Today,* March 1991.

"Child Labor Amendments of 1991." Hearings before the Senate Subcommittee on S.600, March 19, 1991.

"Child Labor in the World Today." *UNESCO Courier,* October 1991.

"Children at Risk in the Workplace." Hearings before the Employment and Housing Subcommittee, 101st Congress, March 16 and June 8, 1990.

Children's Defense Fund. *Child Poverty in America.* Washington, D.C.: 1991.

Coldham, Peter Wilson. *Emigrants in Chains, 1607–1776.* Baltimore: Genealogical Publishing, 1992.

Cole, Paul C. *Children At Work: Peril or Promise?* Albany, NY: New York State AFL-CIO, 1991.

Commons, John R., and Associates. *History of Labor in the U.S.* (Vol. 1). New York: Macmillan, 1918.

Congressional Research Service. *Child Day Care* (CRS Info Pack). Washington, D.C.: Library of Congress, 1991.

―――. *Child Abuse and Neglect.* (CRS Info Pack). Washington, D.C.: Library of Congress, 1991.

"Continuing Oversight of Children at Risk in the Workplace." Hearing before the Employment and Housing Subcommittee, 101st Congress, August 7, 1991.

Davis, Allen F., and Mary Lynn McCree. *80 Years at Hull House.* Chicago: Quadrangle, 1969.

Dunbar, Tony. *Our Land Too.* New York: Pantheon, 1971.

"Environmental Toxins and Children: Exploring the Risks" (Parts I and II). Hearings before the Select Committee on Children, Youth and Families, 101st Congress, Sept. 6, 1990.

Fried, Albert, ed. *Except to Walk Free: Documents and Notes in the History of American Labor.* New York: Anchor, 1974.

"A Future Denied: Children Who Work," UN Chronicle, September 1989.

Gibbs, N. R. "Suffer the Little Children." *Time,* March 26, 1990.

Greene, Janet W. *Child Labor in New York State: Indentured Servants in the Colonial Era.* Troy, New York: Sage, 1991.

Greider, William. *Who Will Tell the People? The Betrayal of American Democracy*. New York: Simon & Schuster, 1992.

Gutman, Herbert G. *Work, Culture and Society in Industrialized America*. New York: Knopf, 1976.

Hill, Robert B., and Regina Nixon. *Youth Employment in American Industry*. Washington, D.C.: National Urban League, 1984.

Hoffman, Michael A., II. *They Were White and They Were Slaves*. Dresden, New York: Wiswell Ruffin, 1991.

Hunter, Robert. *Poverty*. New York: Macmillan, 1904.

Inglis, Brian. *Men of Conscience*. New York: Macmillan, 1971.

Innes, Stephen, ed. *Work and Labor in Early America*. Chapel Hill, North Carolina: University of North Carolina Press, 1988.

Job Smarts. Washington, D.C.: U.S. Department of Labor and National Child Labor Committee, n.d.

Johnson, Clifford M., et al. *Child Poverty in America*. Washington, DC: Children's Defense Fund, 1991.

Kinkead, Gwen. "Chinatown." *New Yorker,* June 10, 1991.

Knowledge Is Power: Teenagers and Their Parents Need to Know About Teenage Jobs. Chicago: National Safe Workplace Institute, n.d.

Kozol, Jonathan. "If We Want to Change Our Schools," *Rethinking Schools,* March–April 1992.

Labor Legacy Committee. *The Working Teenager*. Albany: New York State AFL-CIO, 1989.

Lantos, Tom. "The Silence of the Kids: Children at Risk in the Workplace." *Labor Law Journal,* February 1992.

Larkin, Jack. *The Reshaping of Everyday Life, 1790–1840*. New York: Harper and Row, 1988.

Lifetime Television. *Your Family Matters: Danger, Kids at Work*. 1991.

London, Jack. *The People of the Abyss*. Westport, Connecticut: Lawrence Hill, 1977.

Lumpkin, Katharine DePre, and Dorothy W. Douglas. *Child Workers in America*. New York: International, 1937.

Markham, Edwin. *Children in Bondage*. Philadelphia: Ayer, 1964.

Meltzer, Milton. *Bread—And Roses: The Struggle of American Labor, 1865–1915*. New York: Facts on File, 1991.

———. *Slavery: A World History*. New York: Da Capo, 1993.

———. *Taking Root: Jewish Immigrants in America.* New York: Farrar, Straus, & Giroux, 1976.

Miller, Marc S., ed. *Working Lives.* New York: Pantheon, 1980.

Nardinelli, Clark. *Child Labor and the Industrial Revolution.* Bloomington: Indiana University Press, 1990.

National Safe Workplace Institute. "America's Unseen Education Crisis: Student-Workers' Need to Balance Work and Academic/Personal Development in Their Lives." May 12, 1992.

Olson, Tod, "Robbed of a Childhood." *Scholastic Update,* January 25, 1991.

Phillips, Kevin, *The Politics of Rich and Poor.* New York: HarperCollins, 1991.

Pollack, Susan H., and Philip J. Landrigan. "Child Labor in 1990: Prevalence and Health Hazards." *Annual Review of Public Health,* 1990.

Poole, Ernest. "Child Labor: The Street" and "Child Labor: Factories and Stores." *Annals of the American Academy,* May 1905.

Pope, Liston. *Millhands and Preachers.* New Haven, Connecticut: Yale University Press, 1942.

Ross, Steven J. *Workers on the Edge: Work, Leisure and Politics in Industrializing Cincinnati, 1788–1890.* New York: Columbia University Press, 1985.

Simons, Janet M., Belva Finlay, and Alice Young. *The Adolescent and Young Adult Fact Book.* Washington, D.C.: Children's Defense Fund, 1991.

Simonson, Joy R. "Summary Comparison of Current and Pending Child Labor Legislation." Prepared for Lantos House Committee, May 21, 1992.

Snedeker, Bonnie. *Hard Knocks: Preparing Youth for Work.* Baltimore: Johns Hopkins University Press, 1982.

Spargo, John. *The Bitter Cry of the Children.* Chicago: Quadrangle, 1968.

Stein, Leon. *The Triangle Fire.* Philadelphia: Lippincott, 1962.

Steinberg, Lawrence, and Allen Greensberger. *When Teenagers Work: The Psychological and Social Costs of Adolescent Employment.* New York: Basic Books, 1986.

Sterling, Dorothy, ed. *We Are Your Sisters: Black Women in the Nineteenth Century.* New York: Norton, 1984.

Still So Far to Go: Child Labor in the World Today. Geneva, Switzerland: International Labor Organization, 1989.

Swados, Harvey, ed. *Years of Conscience: The Muckrakers.* Cleveland: World, 1962.

Tax, Meredith. *The Rising of the Women, 1880–1917.* New York: Monthly Review, 1980.

Training Opportunities in the Job Corps: A Directory of Job Corps Centers and Courses. Washington, DC: U.S. Department of Labor, 1990.

UN Children's Fund. *The State of the World's Children, 1991.* New York: United Nations, 1990.

West, Elliott, and Paula Petrik, eds. *Small Worlds: Children and Adolescents in America, 1850–1950.* Lawrence: University Press of Kansas, 1992.

Whittaker, William. *Child Labor: Issues for the 102nd Congress.* Washington, DC: U.S. Government Printing Office, 1992.

Woodward, C. Vann. *Origins of the New South, 1877–1913.* Baton Rouge: Louisiana State University Press, 1951.

Working America's Children to Death. American Youth Work Center and National Consumers League, n.d.

Working Teenager. Albany: New York State Department of Labor, n.d.

Zinn, Howard. *A People's History of the United States.* New York: Harper and Row, 1980.

Source Notes

In the following list, sources relied on for aspects of each chapter are singled out, by the last name of the author. For publication details, see the bibliography.

Chapter 1: Meltzer's world history of slavery for the work of children in bondage in the ancient and medieval worlds. Bremner's monumental documentary history was of inestimable value in this and the next five chapters. I also used Spargo, Hoffman, Bailyn, Greene, and Cole.

Chapter 2: Bremner, Sterling, Greene, and Meltzer contain many documents on the lot of African American children during slavery times.

Chapter 3: Battiscombe's richly detailed life of the British reformer Shaftsbury was very helpful on the early industrial revolution. I also used Coldham, Spargo, and Hoffman.

Chapter 4: Bremner again, for several of the documentary passages, and Larkin for the early American industrial experience. Commons's massive four-volume history of American labor, a pioneering classic, was helpful, too.

Chapter 5: Ross's intensive study of industrial growth in a midwestern city was the source of the Cincinnati section. Tax, Spargo, Zinn, Gutman, Swados, and Bremner all contributed details or documents.

Chapter 6: Turn-of-the-century documentation on child labor came from Spargo, Woodward, Pope, and London. For the thirties, I relied on Lumpkin and Douglas, whose book is both scholarly and moving for its first-person investigation of young workers in the early Depression years. The minutely detailed list of tasks was compiled by them.

Chapter 7: The reform movement is documented in Swados, the Triangle fire in Stein, the evolution of labor law in Brock, Lumpkin, Lantos, Pope, Whittacker, Spargo, and the congressional hearings.

Chapter 8: For "Operation Child Watch" I used Bingham, Gibbs, the *New York Times,* and congressional testimony. The Landrigan statement is from the *New York Times* of June 26, 1992. Mayo's testimony is from congressional hearings, and so are the quotes dealing with the fast food chains.

Chapter 9: The opening passage on today's sweatshops is based on an interview with Jeffrey Newman, director of the National Child Labor Committee. A congressional hearing provided the eyewitness account of a Bronx sweatshop. Recent Chinese immigration is based on a *New York Times* report of March 21, 1992. The sweatshops in New York's Chinatown are described by Gwen Kinkead in the *New Yorker* of June 10, 1991, and in the *Village Voice* of February 5, 1991. Dr. Landrigan's statement was made at a congressional hearing on March 26, 1989. Augustine Nieves and William Hoerger testified at a congressional hearing on August 7, 1991. The way in which unlicensed farm labor contractors operate was described at a hearing before Senator Howard Metzenbaum's subcommittee. Dr. Monahan testified at the same hearing. The testimony of Marilyn Adams and Otto Petersen is from a transcript of the Lifetime TV program of 1991. The effect of farm labor on children's health comes from hearings of the Metzenbaum committee on March 19, 1991.

Chapter 10: Jennifer Forshee told of her accident at a House committee hearing on August 7, 1991. How Jesse Colton died was described by his mother to the Lantos Subcommittee on March 16, 1990. Matthew Garvey testified at the same hearing, as did the parents of Michael Hucorne. Joseph Curley told of his son Kevin's death at a hearing of the Lantos Subcommittee on June 8, 1990. Discussion of health hazards in child labor is based on Pollack and Landrigan. The link between injury rates and child labor was demonstrated in hearings of Senator Metzenbaum's committee.

Chapter 11: Interference with school performance is documented in Cole and in Pollack and Landrigan. The program of Junior Achievement is described in its annual reports. Information on the European work-study programs and comparison with the American is given in the *Nation* of March 16, 1992. The Hobart proposal is described in Cole. The needs of minority youth were assessed in the *New York Times* of June 7, 1992. The Job Corps projects are listed in that agency's annual reports. The Gordon Berlin quote comes from the *New York Times* of February 12, 1992.

Chapter 12: The facts on young Mexicans working in American-owned enterprises below the border come from Greider, a superbly documented investigation of the realities of corporate and political power in America. Child labor in other parts of the world is documented in Whittaker, "Child Labor in the World Today," "A Future Denied," and in UN Children's Fund publications, as well as in hearings on March 19, 1991, of the Metzenbaum committee. *Newsweek* on May 4, 1992, reported on the enslavement of children in the world today.

Chapter 13: Poverty among children today is documented in Johnson and in other publications of the Children's Defense Fund. The suggestions on what might be done to eliminate child labor or at least to lessen the exploitation of children who work are based on my own response to a great variety of proposals made by politicians, economists, sociologists, and the organizations that devote themselves to the welfare of children.

Chapter 14: Much of the information for the questions and answers is taken from *Knowledge Is Power,* a brochure of the National Safe Workplace Institute, Chicago, and from *Job Smarts,* a brochure issued jointly by the U.S. Department of Labor and the National Child Labor Committee.

Index